T0149071

THIS
WORLD
BELOW
ZERO
FAHRENHEIT

THIS
WORLD
BELOW
ZERO
FAHRENHEIT

Travels in the
Kashmir Valley

SUHAS MUNSHI

VINTAGE
An imprint of Penguin Random House

VINTAGE

USA | Canada | UK | Ireland | Australia
New Zealand | India | South Africa | China

Vintage is part of the Penguin Random House group of companies
whose addresses can be found at global.penguinrandomhouse.com

Published by Penguin Random House India Pvt. Ltd
7th Floor, Infinity Tower C, DLF Cyber City,
Gurgaon 122 002, Haryana, India

Penguin
Random House
India

First published in Vintage by Penguin Random House India 2021

Copyright © Suhas Munshi 2021

All rights reserved

10 9 8 7 6 5 4 3 2 1

ISBN 9780670091959

Typeset in Minion Pro by Manipal Technologies Limited, Manipal
Printed at Replika Press Pvt. Ltd, India

www.penguin.co.in

*For my family and friends,
and for Sana*

Contents

Introduction

'This is not a goddamn "Heaven".'

Many years ago, a close friend called me up, fuming at a run-of-the-mill piece on Kashmir. 'Why do they keep saying it? We live here. We are not dead yet.' I knew what he meant. The cliché wasn't just off-putting. It was corrosive. It reduced a living place to an amusement park. 'Heaven'. When Kashmir wasn't that it was a 'geostrategic' something or a 'battleground xxx'. Every time such a cliché was uttered, Kashmir and its people grew a little more distant, more abstract. My friend's words remained somewhere at the back of my mind. Which is why I couldn't help but share a chance encounter I had with a Kashmiri man returning from a regular nine-to-five shift. And the conversations I had with elderly football enthusiasts, actors, poets, shepherds and ambitious young men and women, some of whom were fighting for their identities like people anywhere else in the world. To them Kashmir was only a home, with all its imperfections.

To Ali Mohammad, a cobbler who has been sitting in front of the old Tyndale-Biscoe School at Lal Chowk for the past twenty-five years, it is the 'best place in the whole wide world'. Though, by his own admission, he has never travelled beyond Jammu. He likes it despite the fact that in these twenty-five years, 'a lot of people who used to push carts for a living have now become very rich. Some of them are even driven to their shops in expensive cars. It hurts because the place where I sit, my brother-in-law sat for fifty years before me. Fifty plus twenty-five is how much?'

Seventy-five.

'Exactly. For the last seventy-five years, we have been sitting in this corner of the road mending and polishing shoes. What do we have to show for it? Just a two-room house in Batmaloo.' He blames it on his stingy customers, the *Shikaslads* [which means the bringer of misfortune and is often used as a term of mild abuse], whom nothing can cure, 'not even the air of Lal Chowk, which our elders would say was the remedy to all ills.'

When I started work on this book, a little over two years ago, I did not have any grand, connecting theme in mind. I only knew what I was not going to write about—violence (and I failed even at that). The moment it became central to any story, violence had a tendency of eclipsing everything else. The best way to deal with it was probably through allusion. Something of the sort that had been done in *Valley of Saints*, a movie on Kashmir, set in Kashmir, which had won many international awards, including two at the Sundance film festival. There's a scene in it in which a character, Afzal, is trying to cheer up his friend Gulzar. As they're lying in bed, Afzal thinks of an act—mimicking corpses. The way a person looks in death depends on the way they die, Afzal says. He plays the part of a person who has been shot to death—limbs bent at unnatural angles, a bit of flesh showing around the waist. It's as if in that frame, for a second, he becomes, at once, all the people who were gunned down in the valley.

I met and wrote about Afzal, whose real name is also Afzal. We talked about the big international film festivals he had attended, his passion for films and for teaching film-making to his college students. Then he mentioned one day of his life, every second of which he said he remembered with absolute clarity. It was the day when he saw his father's body disfigured by bullets. This was in the early 1990s, when Afzal was only thirteen years old. He grew up in what was one of the most traumatic periods in Kashmir's history. Like him, a lot of other people I spoke to for this book had grown up seeing their lives fall to pieces. The one thing I was determined to avoid kept catching up with me everywhere I went in Kashmir.

But there were moments of joy and love as well, such as those I experienced in a church in north Kashmir on Christmas eve, when there was nothing as dangerous for miles around as the freezing cold. And sometimes it got even better. That bright, sunny day, for instance, when I was in south Kashmir sitting with an old Kashmiri Pandit, O.N. Bhat, as he recalled stories from his childhood. One of them was about Mahatma Gandhi's visit to Kashmir. According to Bhat, Gandhi had delivered a speech about the poverty of the ordinary Kashmiri who 'was so broke he could not even afford a *langot* [loincloth].' 'Langot,' repeated Bhat. It was really funny how he said it. We couldn't stop laughing for a long time.

The place where he lives, Hal in Shopian, was once home to around 100 Pandit families. All of them fled the valley to escape religious persecution. From the window of his first-floor bedroom, Bhat can see the abandoned houses crumbling under their own weight. What used to be his living, thriving neighbourhood is a ghost town today. His is a strange kind of exile. Despite having stayed, he's as far from his home—the one in which he grew up, got married, started a family—as my grandparents, who had to, very late in their lives, leave the houses that they had put together brick by brick, and anchor their families in strange lands. They loved to talk about their lives before the exodus. It often started with someone asking, 'Do you remember . . .' and a whole night would pass just like that.

Daniel Mendelsohn, the great essayist, in 'An Odyssey' describes the genesis of the word 'nostalgia'. One of its roots is Nostos, the Greek word for "homecoming".

In time this wistful word nostos, rooted so deeply in the
Odyssey's themes, was eventually combined with another word
in Greek's vast vocabulary of pain, algos, to give us an elegantly
simple way to talk about the bittersweet feeling we sometimes
have for a special kind of troubling longing. Literally this word
means 'the pain associated with longing for home,' but as we
know, 'home,' particularly as we get older, can be a time as well
as a place.

It really surprised me, when I first went through the finished
draft, to find that I had spoken to and written about so many old
people. I'm not sure what the reason was for this. Maybe in trying
to avoid writing about pain and anxiety and physical hurt, with
which the valley is brimming right now, I was drawn towards a
time when Kashmiris took their lives more or less for granted, and
only our elderly knew what it was like then. Also, there was no
doubt that these links to our shared history weren't going to be
around forever. The memory of Ghulam Rasool Dar or 'Lassa', for
example, who has lived such an eventful life, is already failing him.

I met him on his boat, 'Stranger in Paradise'. It was the last
interview I did for the book. When I met him, he insisted that we
speak only in English. He had an impressive grasp of the language
despite never having been to a school. 'I been working as a *shikara*
man for last fifty-two years,' he said. He recalled taking Pandit Ravi
Shankar and George Harrison for boat rides on the Dal. 'I think it
was 1966. It was like a dream. Both of them used to go with me for
boating. Both of them smoked a lot.' He met the famous Bollywood
actor Dilip Kumar, whose wife, he said, 'was very scared of water.
She stayed separately. Dilip Kumar stayed here, in our houseboat
on the Dal.' He talked about helping out many documentary film-
makers and journalists. 'Michael Palin also came here. You can
watch his documentary. I am in it,' he said. I looked it up on the
net. Lassa is really there, sitting in a shikara, chatting with one of
the Monty Pythons!

'There was this other journalist, very big name, you know him? I travelled with him when he came here . . . you know, the one who shot photo of Afghan girl?'

'Oh, yes . . . that Afghan girl with blue eyes,' I said.

'Green eyes. The girl with green eyes,' he corrected me and smiled. It was funny what the brain retained and what it let go after so many years.

I wished him well and excused myself just as a young couple, whom we hadn't noticed arriving, started negotiating with Lassa and a fellow boatman the price of a ride along the Dal. I heard the young boy quote a sum. The other boatman, in that amusing Kashmiri colloquialism—in which the speaker, like an expert classical singer, sets his sentence to a rhythm and raises the pitch of the penultimate syllable so that both the listener and speaker arrive at the last word, the final beat of the rhythm, together—said no. *Would you believe it*, I thought to myself, *there's such elegance even in the way we say no*!

My journeys for this book took me to the beautiful spring of Verinag in the south to Habba Khatoon's relic up north in Gurez, which an English mountain climber, in an account written more than a hundred years ago, described as being exactly like Switzerland, even in its smell. The claim was endorsed by a seasoned Bakarwal nomad shepherd who said Gurez was 'not of this world'.

I spent an unforgettable three weeks with him and his family while they were migrating from Kashmir to Jammu. Living with them taught me so much—among other things, about what it meant to be poor. I never knew the hunger that comes from not being able to afford food. A few days before I moved in with them, I saw another group of Bakarwals with their herd of sheep and goats, bringing traffic on Srinagar's Boulevard Road to a halt. I remember feeling quite sorry for myself when I saw the dusty shepherds trying to move their herd to one side of the road. *What was I getting myself into?*

Even a while after joining the family of Bakarwals, I felt ashamed at the possibility of being seen with them. But that only lasted till my belly was full and my limbs were not sore with exertion. Very soon hunger and fatigue had an equalizing effect. And from thereon I lost count of the times my hosts saved my life, fed me, made me a part of their families, and shared their dreams and their secrets with me. Frankly, I don't even know why they took me in. And I'm not sure how I would react if a perfect stranger landed at my doorstep and expressed his desire to live with my family.

The Bakarwals live an incredibly tough life—carrying entire households up and down mountains, exposing themselves to pretty harsh weather, not sleeping for the fear of thieves, and still losing their herd to them. I asked them why they hadn't opted out. Their way of life isn't easy, yes, but they do not want to work for someone else. The Bakarwals are free people, my hosts said, that's how it has always been.

When I first went there for this book, Kashmir was still part of the state of Jammu and Kashmir, which used to have its own prime ministers well before it had its chief ministers. And before the prime ministers came in, Kashmir was part of a princely state, with its own maharaja. Somewhere in between my travels—while I was returning from Gurez to Srinagar, to be precise—Kashmir was turned into a Union Territory. Who knows what it will become in a few years' time? Give it any name you want. Just don't call it a goddamn 'Heaven'.

NORTH KASHMIR

1

Gurez: In the Shadow of the Moon

It wasn't the best time to leave for Gurez. In less than twenty-four hours, unprecedented restrictions would be imposed in Kashmir and its special status revoked. But in those moments, you couldn't say anything for sure. You could only guess, from looking at the endless convoy of military trucks, that something big was about to happen.[1]

Non-locals, including outstation students and daily-wage labourers, were lining up for cabs bound for Jammu. There were taxis speeding towards the Srinagar airport full of tourists, some of whom, for not abiding by government advisories to leave the valley, had been fished out of their houseboats and hotels and put on the way home. Except for the locals, who couldn't go anywhere, the entire valley was emptying out.

There were obvious challenges to travelling up north from Srinagar. If we were going to war with Pakistan, which was one of the rumours doing the rounds, then Gurez, a border town, would be a rough spot to be stuck in. At any rate, whatever was about to happen would certainly make the 300 km round trip quite difficult. I called up a friend who knew some people in the administration. 'I will not advise it. Curfew could be imposed any minute now, and once it is enforced, not even I will be able to move an inch. Also, your phone won't work there,' he said.

But if the entire state was going to be placed under strict curfew, I argued with myself, I would have to wait indefinitely for civilian traffic to be allowed on the roads again. And if my plan was put off by a couple of months, it would start snowing and then the only road to the remote town of Gurez would vanish for the following six months.

It didn't take much time to reach Bandipora, which is almost halfway between Srinagar and Gurez. The atmosphere at the taxi stands was unusually hushed. Even casual conversations between passengers and drivers were held in whispers. At Bandipora, most of the passengers—and there were just enough to fill a lone taxi— were on their way home. Given how the tension had been building up for weeks, most Kashmiris had already reached places where they could sit tight for a long time. Among those in the taxi, some were making their way with toys for their children, and others with heaps of luggage.

At a corner of the Bandipora taxi stand, an old man in tattered clothes was surrounded by taxi drivers. He was smiling to himself. 'He doesn't remember why he was here or who he is. The only thing he remembers is that he's from Rajouri. He says he had some money but it was stolen yesterday. He was selling his blanket to afford the trip back home. So we're collecting some money for him,' said my Gurez-bound taxi driver. For someone who had lost his memory and all his money, the man looked oddly content. 'You have enough money now. Don't sell your blanket. You'll die of the cold,' a taxi driver instructed him like a schoolmaster while handing over the money. The old man nodded obediently.

I, on the other hand, couldn't stop thinking about the reasons I had come so far. Was it even worth all this trouble? Having found a seat at the back of the shared cab that was now grinding up the hills, I tried to go through my Gurez checklist one last time.

To begin with, there was a claim—made by travellers from the valley as well as other continents—that Gurez was the most beautiful place in Kashmir. There was no way I was going to let it pass unchecked.

I had once asked an old Bakarwal with whom I had spent some time to name his favourite place in the valley. I valued his opinion highly because being a nomadic shepherd, he had seen Kashmir like no one else had—on foot, through summers, winters, autumns and springs, over many decades. 'Gurez,' he had said without a moment's pause. 'There is no place like it. That valley, with its mountains and its river . . . it's not of this world.'

He was not the only one to believe this. Many travellers over the last two centuries had gone to great lengths to describe the beauty of Gurez. Walter Roper Lawrence, a high-ranking officer of the Raj deputed to Kashmir, had described it in these words in *The Valley of Kashmir*,[2] published in 1895:

> Gurais is a lovely valley five miles in length lying at an elevation of about 8000 feet above the sea. The Kishnganga river flows through it, and on either side tower mountain scarps of indescribable grandeur. Perhaps one of the most beautiful scenes in the whole of Kashmir is the grove of huge poplars through which the traveller enters the Gurais valley.

The British officer couldn't help add that 'the climate is dry and mild' and 'excellent English vegetables can be grown . . .'

Oscar Eckenstein, an English mountain climber, went a step ahead in *The Karakorams and Kashmir*,[3] in which he claimed that Gurez was a scaled-up model of Switzerland. 'Even the smell of the villages is the same,' he wrote in his travelogue.

The other reason for going to Gurez was Habba Khatoon. Gurez is where the famous 'Zoon' ('moon' in Kashmiri) is believed to have wandered into after her husband, the king of Kashmir, Yusuf Shah Chak, was dethroned and imprisoned by the Mughals.

It is in Gurez that one can visit a one-of-a-kind literary memorial, the Habba Khatoon peak, in whose lap she is said to have sat and composed some of her best verses some 500 years ago.

But strangely enough, Gurez doesn't feature in any of her poems. Neither does Yusuf Shah Chak. For all we know, she may never have visited the place, and the story about the Habba Khatoon peak could be a myth. After all, why would a poet maddened by separation from her husband walk for so long and never write poems for him? If she indeed made it as far as Gurez, why wouldn't she write about the journey or describe the place where she sat and composed her poems?

All of it sounds implausible, and then I further discover that there exists more than one Habba Khatoon. There is in fact a troop of them. Each telling her own story to her own audience. In some tellings, she's an illiterate peasant, in others she's a learned poet; in some she is born in the fields of South Kashmir, in others she's said to be from around these parts; in some she enjoys royal patronage until her death, in others she renounces the world after her husband's imprisonment. There is also a theory that completely does away with the idea of her ever having been alive. According to it she was a character of a popular fable, to which over the years the public imagination lent flesh and blood. Only in Gurez would I have the chance to learn the real Zoon story.

Gurez is also the last big settlement of the Dards, at least in India. Several centuries ago, their home turf stretched all the way from Gilgit Baltistan in the north to Khyber Pakhtunkhwa in the south, in what came to be called Dardistan, where flourished their own language, Shina. But other expanding empires, wars and haphazardly drawn boundaries reduced them to one tiny district. Who knew when even this tiny dot of civilization would disappear altogether?

I could have thought of several other reasons for visiting Gurez, if only the driver had stopped playing Mohammed Aziz.

For three hours, Aziz's diehard fan had played nothing but him on full blast. I lost count of the number of times we heard '*Kahan aa gaye hum, kahan kho gaye hum*'. In its last few iterations, the song, like creeping madness, had even begun making sense. A few more loops and I probably would have ended up like that old man in the Bandipora taxi stand.

But in the final stretch, with a few kilometres to go, the driver suddenly silenced the music system, probably dizzy with its effects himself. The world outside was beautiful again. Actually, it was turning into something more than that. It was becoming unforgettable.

A bend in the mountain road provided an excellent vantage point from which I could see, far below towards my right, a huge crystal lake. It was surrounded on all sides by tall mountains that were glowing in all possible shades of green. Some were still enveloped in snow. It wasn't hard to guess why Eckenstein would compare Gurez to Swiss villages or why Habba Khatoon wouldn't go anywhere else with her broken heart.

Gurez has, apart from its natural charms, an element that doesn't exist in any other part of Kashmir—distance, both in time and space, from the outside world. Except for an early Buddhist council that some say happened in Kanzalwan, Gurez is not known for hosting any significant religious, political or historical event. It is remarkably austere in that way. It doesn't offer the metropolitan chaos of Srinagar, the profuse hospitality of Pahalgam or the soaring 'Gondolas' of Gulmarg. Like a resolved hermit, it has maintained distance from everything—theology, catastrophes, discoveries, current affairs. The rest of Kashmir, seething with anger and anxiety, may, for all practical purposes, have been 10,000 miles away, on a different continent. It didn't disturb the still air of Gurez.

A young fellow passenger who had been on his phone for half an hour concluded his conversation with great satisfaction. This was clear from the way he locked and tucked in his phone and looked up at me with an ear-to-ear grin. He was brimming with excitement and wanted to chat.

'So you are a journalist?' He had heard me say so to soldiers deployed at over a dozen verification checkpoints we had crossed on the way from Bandipora.

'Yeah, I'm sort of doing some research. So what do you do?'

'I'm a paramedic. You heard the story about the Pakistani boy who drowned in the river, whose body drifted down here and was handed over to Pakistan?'

It was a news item from July about a young Pakistani boy who had slipped and drowned in the Kishenganga, and whose body, after some bureaucratic wrangling, was handed over to the Pakistani army. I told him I had seen it in the news.

'I was the one who discovered the body of that boy. It was in bad shape,' he said proudly. I did not know what to make of it. I asked him if such things happened often.

'Yes, once in a while our people get drowned in the river and end up on that side and their people drown and get washed up on our river banks. But often the armies don't accept bodies like that. People live just a few kilometres apart on either side of the fence but they have to come all the way through New Delhi to collect the bodies. It's a very complex, time-taking procedure. So, what are you researching?'

'Local culture, Habba Khatoon, things like that.'

At the mention of culture and Habba Khatoon, a passenger sitting in front of us turned around. He was a clean-shaven, brightly clothed, heavily built man wearing black shades and thick sideburns that were crawling towards his jawline. He looked like an ageing body double of Elvis Presley. 'Very good, very good. Culture. People need to save culture. All the best. Tell me if you need anything. Anything for culture,' he said, sounding impressed. He introduced himself as a police officer and, turning towards the young boy, started speaking in a strange tongue. Perhaps words of appreciation for the outsider who had come to study their culture and some spiel about how the young boy needed to take more pride in his traditions. They were talking in Shina. This was the first time I had heard it. The language sounded effervescent and full of vigour, like popcorn kernels dancing in a frying pan. Apart from a sprinkling of Urdu and Kashmiri, it was mostly incomprehensible. Shina seemed closer to the tongues of Central Asia.

The police officer was still in the middle of his lecture when we reached the gates of Dawar, behind which rose a huge barren-looking mountain. It stood alone, right in front of us, isolated from the lush green mountains on either side. That solitary rock did not need any introduction. It was the Habba Khatoon peak.

By way of a plan, I did not have anything, only a name: Fareed Kaloo. A friend had given me that name, saying that he ran a theatre group in Habba Khatoon's name and held annual cultural festivals in Gurez. My only hope was to find him somewhere in Gurez. Thankfully, after making a few inquiries, I found him at his house just as he was stepping out.

'Fareed Kaloo?'

'Yes. You are?

My happiness knew no bounds. I gave him my name, the name of my friend, my mission statement, all in quick succession. But he wasn't really paying attention. The kindly looking old man with a trimmed white beard was staring blankly at me, caught, as he was, in the searchlight of my excitement. It took him some time to soak in the sight of a visitor who had arrived at his doorstep unannounced, and was blabbering some nonsense about Habba Khatoon and the endangered culture of the Dards.

'Oh . . . I . . . I was just going to the mosque to offer namaz,' he said after a long pause.

'It's quite fine, Kaloo saahab. I think I'll walk down to the Habba Khatoon mountain meanwhile. That one over there, isn't it?'

'Yes, that's the one. Walk down this road, you'll get to Achoora village. There you'll find Azaad. He'll guide you. By the time you return you'll find me here. You can keep those bags in the room inside.'

I started walking towards the peak. Afterwards, it occurred to me that my tenor was not in keeping with Kaloo saahab's serious demeanour. Instead of the squeals I had let out on seeing him, something more low-key and sombre would have been appropriate. But amends could be made later. For now, the thing to do was to look around and find Habba Khatoon everywhere. From petrol stations to taxi stands and grocery shops, all signboards bore her name. There was even a Habba Khatoon English-medium school.

A few local taxis swished by as I crossed a bridge and left behind the town of Dawar. For the next half-hour, the only sounds I heard were of fast-moving tyres swiftly displacing air, and the chirping of birds. The Kishenganga river and smaller tributaries of it flowed around the road like a braid. The valley was huge. The peaks on both sides were not just tall like skyscrapers, they were immense like the pyramids. Clouds passing above cast dancing shadows on them.

Before describing the grandeur of Gurez in his book, Walter Lawrence wrote a moving passage on the mountains of Kashmir, on which, he said, at different times of the day, you could see shades of violet, purple, indigo, blue, lavender, white, pale bronze, rose, pink, yellow, orange, ruddy crimson and a pale creamy green. And that's not all.

If one were to look downward from the mountains, he adds, 'the valley in the sunshine has the hues of the opal, the pale reds of karewa [dark terraced plateaus], the vivid light greens of the young rice, and the darker shades of the groves of trees relieved by sunlit sheets, gleams of water, and soft blue haze give a combination of tints reminding one irresistibly of the changing hues of that green. It is impossible in the scope of this report to do justice to the beauty and grandeur of the mountains of Kashmir, or to enumerate the lovely glades and forests, visited by so few.'

In the old times, Gurez used to get a lot of visitors. It was a stopover along the ancient Silk Route. Visitors from Gilgit would have to pass through Gurez on their way to Kashgar in China. International traders with long, serpentine chains of attendants bearing sacks of exotic and prized goods may have walked, more or less, on the same path I was walking on then.

It took me about forty-five minutes to reach Achoora, and what felt like twice that time to find Azaad Mapnu. I found him sitting under a tree with some friends.

'Oh, Kaloo saahab has sent you? Please tell me, how can I be of service?' He was a teacher at a local school, probably a few years younger than me. He had graduated from Kashmir University in Srinagar. I asked him whether I was the first person to have come looking for the peak in some time.

'You'll be surprised by the number of people who come here to look at this peak. Only two weeks ago a couple from Tamil Nadu came here. They stayed with me for a few days. They wanted to know everything about her.'

So what was the Habba Khatoon story? I asked him.

'Habba Khatoon was a very beautiful woman and a great poet from a very humble background. She was married to an illiterate moneylender who didn't quite get her literary genius. Then came along the great king, Yusuf Shah Chak, who heard her sing some of her verses while she was working in the fields. He immediately took a liking to her and married Habba Khatoon after forcing the uncouth, ill-tempered moneylender to divorce her. They both lived a very happy and joyous life. Then came the Mughals who destroyed everything. They repeatedly fought against Yusuf Shah Chak and finally managed to defeat him through some conceit and captured him. That's when Habba Khatoon went mad with grief and, wandering through the valleys of Kashmir, landed here. On this very peak she spent a lot of time, writing verses, for her husband.'

But why here of all places in Kashmir?

'She was mad with grief, as I told you. It may not have been a well-thought-out plan. She was looking for her beloved everywhere. This was one of the places. But you know what? She actually found him here. Our elders tell us that Yusuf Chak had made a secret compact with the Mughals and sometimes they would release him from captivity and he would quietly come all the way here and they would meet in complete secrecy.'

'Do you believe this story?' I asked.

'Well, it has travelled through generations. It may not be entirely false.'

Mapnu had taken me up to a spring concealed behind some bushes. This was the Habba Khatoon spring. 'She was carrying a pot of water on her head once and in a fit of anger, given all her miseries, she threw it on this rock over here, giving birth to this spring. The unusual thing about this spring is that it produces warm water during winters and cold water during summers. Quite a thing, isn't it? Nobody has been able to find its source yet,' he said, waiting for me to touch the water and verify his claims. 'Yes, it's quite cold,' I said with some enthusiasm. I asked him if the mountain had always looked this barren and desolate. Yes, yes, it did.

I asked him about life here in Gurez, and whether it felt too limiting for someone like him who had studied in a university outside. Did he ever wish to move out to a better life?

'I don't how it will sound to you, but if you look at the houses around, look at the clothes people are wearing, how they're spending their time, you'll realize that the people here have still not learnt the ways of the world and they're quite content with what they have. Yes, I have been outside my village. I have seen a little of the life outside. But I like my home more than any other place in the world. I made a conscious choice to remain here in Achoora and teach our children, instead of trying to find a better paying job outside. You won't find any malice in people here. There are hardships, of course, the whole place gets barricaded by snow for six months. We can't move outside our houses during that time. There are emergencies, medical emergencies when we have to request the forces to fly people out in their choppers. It is still very inconvenient for us. It is tough to keep oneself warm during those months. But we still are where we've always been. In the shadow of Habba Khatoon,' he said, pointing towards the mountain that we were now leaving behind.

It was almost sunset and a light drizzle had started. I wished him well and started walking briskly back to Dawar. The mountain itself was dark now, except for its summit, which was brightly lit by the dying rays of the sun.

'In the shadow of Habba Khatoon.' It was a neat phrase. Habba Khatoon did not have the readership of other poets such as Lal Ded, though her stature and contribution to Kashmiri culture was no less. If Lal Ded had started a movement of religious reform, one hundred years before Kabir, and spoken of things that were on everyone's mind—exploitation by religious heads, the tyranny of rituals—but which nobody had the courage to utter, Habba Khatoon went a step further and said things that were on everyone's minds—the desire for fulfilment, the right to be treated with equal respect—but which nobody, the men especially, had the courage to hear.

Neerja Mattoo in her book *The Mystic and the Lyric: Four Women Poets of Kashmir*[4] calls Habba Khatoon and Arnimal, who was born some two hundred years later, 'the original feminists'. She also translates some of Habba Khatoon's unforgettable verses.

Verses that are full of playful love, such as this:

From the window he looked at me
The long-necked beauty that I am
My heart he left bereft
How he fills me with longing for him!

Verses of outburst:

> The birth of a daughter snares you in a web
> The birth of a daughter is a smear on your name
> A lion you may be, but a jackal you become.
> Wake up my jewel, from your sleep.

And of hopelessness:

> The world is nothing but misery, O mynah!
> Nothing will last, not even a memory
> Mynah, the world's a miserable place
> Nothing will last, not a memory.

Her lyrics did not just last. They flourished. Women sang them while working in the fields. They still do. Within the last couple of years, a few artists have sung her 'Roshay' and introduced the Zoon to non-Kashmiri speaking masses.

It was past sunset when I reached Dawar. I was retracing my steps to Kaloo saahab's house when I came across a barber shop. I had been on the road for ten days and felt I could do with a quick shave. The three young boys sitting inside were clearly not from these parts. 'We are from Dhampur, Bijnor, in Uttar Pradesh,' said a boy who introduced himself as Mohammad Umer.

Umer's father had in 2005 come to Bandipora, where he had set up a small tea and *pakora* stall. He worked with his father for a year but after making a trip to Gurez for some work, realized that there were no barbers here. He saw a business opportunity and set up shop.

So what sort of hairstyles were in vogue these days?

'People are very simple here. In Bandipora they wanted all sorts of crazy stuff. Those people think they're smarter than everyone else. Here the maximum they ask for is an L-type sidebrow,' Umer said. All this while we were being amused by the antics of Umer's friend, Vishal, who had also come with him from the northern

Uttar Pradesh town. As I was taking notes, Vishal moved around us miming a video camera with his finger frames.

'So, Vishal,' I turned towards him, 'what do you plan to do here during the next six months?'

'What do you mean?'

'Well, soon the whole place is going to be covered in heavy snow and you won't be able to leave this small town for six months. Surely you know that?'

He let out an expletive. He didn't know.

'Vishal doesn't listen to us,' Umer said. 'The snow here is pretty bad. During peak winter, all we get to eat are some frozen vegetables. There is nothing to do except to sit tight. My sister was here with me some winters ago. She was down with a stomach infection while it was still snowing. It was a miserable time for all of us. Finally, she had to be airlifted to Srinagar.'

It was getting really late. I took my leave. I hadn't taken two steps out of their shop when I bumped into a man. He had heard us talk in Hindi and had come to join in. I apologized to him and told him that I had no time, and would come the next day. He understood. '*Hum* Sitapur *se hain. Chai pakode ki dukaan hai apni. Aaiyega zaruur* [I'm from Sitapur. I run a *chai-pakora* stall. Do come],' he said.

I was finally in the company of Fareed Kaloo. After a round of tea, we came to the subject of Habba Khatoon. So what was his Habba Khatoon story?

'To begin with, she was surely a talented poet and an exceptional singer. If you go through her songs, you'll understand that they're meant to be sung. Also, she was strikingly beautiful. About her particulars, we know that she was from Pampore, that she was married to an illiterate man against her wishes, that one day the then king of Kashmir—Yusuf Shah Chak—was taking a walk near the fields where he heard her singing her songs. He immediately took a liking to her, arranged for her divorce from that boor and got married to her. Upon her marriage to the king, she was crowned as the queen of Kashmir. Habba Khatoon exerted her influence over the king and urged him to be kind and gentle to his subjects. Yusuf Shah Chak was a Shia and his wazir was quite ruthless with their Sunni subjects. One day, the Sunnis decided they had enough. They sent a secret delegation to Mughal emperor Akbar in Delhi and begged him to intervene. Akbar agreed. In his first attack, the Mughal emperor was unsuccessful. But he was victorious in his second attempt. Chak was captured and sent to a prison in Bihar. Habba Khatoon was dethroned. I think she came here for old memories' sake. I think she and Yusuf Shah Chak spent some memorable times here. She was a queen once; she knew that she would never see her husband again. Although it is strange that she has mentioned Wular lake, Dal, Pampore, but never Gurez.'

Why did he think that the songs of Habba Khatoon were still sung so many centuries after her death?

'In Kashmir, winters are terrible. People sit together and talk about this and that during the long nights, since there is no other form of entertainment available to us. One of the favourite subjects is poetry. The elders in our town sit by the fire until the early hours of the morning and recite verses from various poets. Habba Khatoon is among the poets who is recited. She lived not just in the fields, in the voices of women peasants, she has lived here in our houses as well. The winters have kept her memory alive.'

I thought it remarkable that the most famous cultural icon in the land of the Shinas/Dards was a person from south Kashmir. I told him so.

He laughed like old people do, without any reserve, full of warmth. 'She is the *bahu* [daughter-in-law] of Dardistan. She may not have spoken our tongue but she is family.'

What did he make of the shrinking Dard population?

'It seems in hindsight very arbitrary, the things that have happened to us. Our relations with our families were severed after Partition. The area where you went today, Achoora and villages beyond it, was once part of Pakistan. In Achoora, their army had actually set up headquarters for one of their battalions. But a year after Partition, India took over that land. So it became India's territory. We regained some of our relations. Habba Khatoon peak also was ours again. So I don't know, hundreds of years from now, where we will be. And God knows what will happen to our language. You know I talk to my son in Kashmiri at home now so that he has better prospects when he goes out to the valley in search of a job or education.' I couldn't help but think about how my own parents, after migrating to Delhi, had started speaking to me in Hindi and English for the same reasons.

It was quite late, sometime past midnight, when we decided to finish our dinner and hit our beds. I borrowed his phone to call my wife, to tell her that I was doing fine. But there was no signal on his phone either. Kaloo said that the network was often patchy in these parts, and there was no need to worry. We slept.

But I kept waking up and checking Kaloo's phone. The network had not returned. Something didn't feel right. At about six in the morning, I decided to pack my bags. I left Kaloo's house as abruptly as I had entered it. This was the dawn of 5 August 2019.

A cab driver at Dawar's taxi stand was waiting to get three more passengers. I checked with the other passengers. Nobody's phones were working. I paid the amount for two extra passengers and we left. Midway through the journey, at a tea stall where we took a break, a man said India and Pakistan had gone to war. He said he had seen heavy artillery move towards the border. 'War has broken out. That's what has happened,' he said, guffawing. He was an ambulance driver. 'Try as you might, you'll never be able to get out of here. They'll stop you shortly before Bandipora. They only let me come up because of an emergency.'

He was correct. Our car, which was the first passenger vehicle to come down that day from Gurez, was stopped near a security camp. The soldiers said they couldn't let us proceed without the approval of their seniors. I asked the soldiers if they had a phone. Nobody did. If indeed war had broken out, and my family wasn't able to get in touch with me, I only hoped that they hadn't switched on their television sets yet. After half an hour, we were allowed to move ahead but only till the next security camp, which was not far from the Bandipora taxi stand, from where I was hoping to get a cab back to Srinagar. By then all the passengers, except one, had decided to go back to Gurez, not wanting to be stranded in a place from where a return journey would become impossible. We were dropped a few kilometres short of our destination at a little past 10 a.m. From there, we started towards Bandipora on foot.

The taxi stand, the markets, the whole town looked deserted. The roads and alleys were full of armed security men. My fellow traveller, who said he was from Gurez and claimed to know these parts well, asked me to keep my head down and continue walking. But I couldn't help asking a man who was selling cigarettes behind a half-open shutter and watching television what had happened. 'They've finished 370,' he said, referring to the nullification of Article 370 of the Indian Constitution which gave special status to Jammu and Kashmir. 'And?' I asked, not sure if all the build-up over the past month was over this one decision. 'We don't have time. We need to keep moving,' the Gurezi said.

A little further down when we crossed the town, he gave some more details about himself. He was a soldier in a paramilitary force and was returning to his unit after spending some time at his home. He had been caught in a similar situation back in 2016 when a young militant named Burhan Wani was killed in an encounter, and widespread protests had broken out across the valley. He had to foot the journey till Srinagar. 'Looks like the same thing. If we walk quickly, we might be able to reach Srinagar by around seven,' he said. Between the two of us, in that hostile atmosphere, I think he felt far more vulnerable, and for good reason.

Almost two years earlier, a senior police officer had been lynched in downtown Srinagar. At about the same time, a Kashmiri army officer who was visiting his home in the valley was killed.

Kashmiris serving in the forces were scared for their lives and for the lives of their families. But it wasn't a recent phenomenon.

I had, as it happens, been on a similar journey on foot with another person dressed in civvies back in February 2013. A Kashmiri man, Afzal Guru, had been hung for plotting a terror attack on the Indian Parliament. Soon after his hanging, curfew had been imposed across Kashmir. A friend and I were travelling in a taxi from Srinagar to Baramulla when, somewhere around Pattan, the car right in front of us was attacked with stones by some masked teenagers. They did not want any vehicles on that road. The three of us—my friend, our fellow passenger and I—walked all the way to Baramulla. Only after we had reached the town did the man with us show us photos of his unit on his mobile and tell us who he really was—a policeman too scared to visit his home in his uniform.

It was a warm, sunny day. After an hour of walking and sweating it out, we finally got a ride. The Gurezi had waved down a car whose driver was headed towards Sumbal, around 40 kilometres before Srinagar, and didn't mind our company. It is astonishing that in a place like Kashmir, where such a long-drawn-out conflict has begotten a silent army of informants and sowed mistrust even within families, people are still willing to open their doors to strangers.

'What's happening?' we asked him. He did not know anything. The Gurezi, a man of few words, suddenly turned into a carefree, talkative person, and struck a chord with the driver. Seated behind, I was introduced as a scholar from New Delhi who was trying to get to the airport and on the first flight out of Kashmir.

'*Tum log hame chhod ke jaa rahe ho. Dekhna ye log hame jaan se maar denge* (You people are leaving us behind. These people [security forces] will kill us, you'll see),' the driver said to me. He was laughing, even though his face betrayed his nervousness. 'When all of you go, who will bear witness to things that will happen to us? But if this is God's will, so be it,' he said.

Concertina wires were still being stretched wide across roads that we were driving through. At one security checkpoint, an aggressive, automatic-rifle-bearing soldier stopped our car and asked us for our identification papers. The Gurezi tried to play cool and said he was a soldier.

'Show me your ID.'

'I don't have it. You know that we can't carry around our identification papers on holidays.'

'Then tell me how many female units we have in Kashmir,' he asked while his grip over his gun stiffened. Even the Gurezi, who must have conducted such routine examinations many times himself, was taken aback by the abruptness of the question.

'HOW MANY?' the soldier repeated his question menacingly. 'O-o-one . . . no . . . t-t-two . . . no . . . wait,' the Gurezi stuttered. He finally got it right the third time. 'Minor inconvenience,' he said, wiping the sweat from his brow as we were allowed to go.

We had left Sumbal far behind. At our request, the driver was now trying to get us from the highway into Srinagar through some roads and bylanes that were not yet blocked. We had reached the Batmaloo taxi stand when the Gurezi had the presence of mind to ask the driver to stop. The driver would have continued, for no apparent reason but to help us as much as he could, driving further into Srinagar, while jeopardizing his own safety and the chances of returning to his family in Sumbal. When we alighted from his car and thanked him profusely, the driver offered an apology. 'Back then I said things which may have upset you. Please don't mind. This is after all not your fault. Reach your house safely and take some cash from me. God knows when ATMs will work again,' he said, reaching out for his wallet. I told him that he had already been more than kind to me. I thanked him for bringing us this far.

The first thing the Gurezi did as soon as we resumed our journey on foot towards Lal Chowk was to rush to a small window in the market and ask for kulfi. Magically, two kulfis appeared. 'It's a hot day. We can't go on without it. I know the guy. He's good,' he said, offering me one. I had never seen Srinagar so bereft of people. He hadn't either. The only moving things on those roads apart from us were small, speeding cavalcades of black SUVs.

Near a police compound, we heard a woman crying loudly. Her wails and shrieks were the only sounds you could hear in that otherwise silent city. A policeman told us that she had just been informed that her son had died some 30 kilometres away in a traffic collision the night before. Since the phones weren't working, this information had taken a lot of time to reach her. And now, given the communication blockade, she didn't know how to fetch her son's body or perform his last rites, as she had no means of contacting her own family. The situation became almost a normal occurrence in the days that followed. People often got to know about the death of their relatives and friends long after they had been laid to rest.

At Lal Chowk, the Gurezi and I parted ways with a handshake. He moved towards his unit, and I headed towards the local press club. I was still trying to process what the shopkeeper in Bandipora had said earlier that day. 'They've finished 370.' What did it mean? It was hard to say in those moments. But what was happening all around, what was clearly visible, was that the Kashmiris had been straitjacketed once again. Mobile connections and Internet access were disconnected across the valley. The few who had access to television through satellite dishes watched people celebrating on news channels. Days passed before Kashmiris could get a sense of what was happening to them, and before the rest of the world could understand what was happening in Kashmir.

For the first few days, a handful of phone booths set up by the administration was the only way for lakhs of local residents to reach out to their family members.[5] People had to walk for several kilometres and wait for hours to be able to get a few minutes on a phone.[6] Even then, many women couldn't get access to phone booths where female security guards weren't deputed to frisk them.[7] People were being brought to hospital with grievous injuries and hospital staff had no way of contacting their families.[8] A twenty-two-year-old boy, who died from snakebite, could have survived had his mother been able to make a call to doctors and arrange the antivenom in time.[9]

Restrictions didn't lead to just medical emergencies or financial setbacks or educational crises. They naturally carried over to personal liberties and private relationships as well. I was thinking about a mother who had told me how her little daughter who lived in another city couldn't sleep without seeing her mummy on video calls every night, about the old men I had met at the TRC stadium who had told me how they made stupid excuses at home just so that they could get together, smoke, laugh and relish football all day long. I remembered the destitute old man I had seen at the Bandipora taxi stand who had lost his memory. Had he reached his home in time?

2

Merry Christmas in Baramulla

The stories I grew up hearing or reading about Baramulla were mostly to do with violence. The earliest was about a nightmarish assault of tribals, from Khyber Pakhtunkhwa and adjoining tribal areas, led by the Pakistani army through Baramulla all the way to the outskirts of Srinagar in October 1947, two months after Partition. The band of marauders had directed their violence—executions, torture and rape, eyewitnesses have said in news reports—at those who could not recite the Kalima.

My first visit to Baramulla many years ago was also marked with violence. Minutes before I entered the city, a confrontation between some stone-throwers and security forces had taken place. Bricks, stones and shattered glass were strewn across what is known as the 'cement bridge'. In *Witness: Kashmir 1986–2016, Nine Photographers*,[1] noted photojournalist Showkat Nanda says that because of the number of people who have died in violent clashes near the 'cement bridge', the angel of death is believed to live there. He shares a personal story about this bridge, of a time when he was covering a clash between security forces and protesters.

Nanda spots a young boy, barely twelve years old, being brought towards him by some other boys. Keeping his camera aside, he takes the boy in his embrace and notices that a bullet has pierced his chest. Nanda describes how he tried to console the boy, how the boy died in his arms, and how, after the protesters had deserted the site, a small child, who someone says was a friend of the dead boy, came out of nowhere to throw stones at paramilitary soldiers and their armoured vehicle.

It was on a late afternoon in December 2019 that I found myself returning to that bridge. I had some time to spare. Those in the markets, the hawkers and buyers, went about their business hurriedly, as if they were making up for lost time. It is difficult to imagine but till a few years before Partition, this town used to be an important stopover between Rawalpindi and Srinagar. It was a gateway of sorts to Kashmir and for those venturing out to Central Asian metropolises like Samarkand and Tashkent. But Partition and the subsequent creation of the Line of Control between India and Pakistan turned Baramulla into a dead-end.

I looked around one last time. On the other side of the bridge, spread out on the mountains far behind, was the old Baramulla town. I looked at the Jhelum flowing below and wondered what a boat trip from Awantipora, south of this place, would have been like. Row for a day, take a break at Srinagar for a couple of days, row more, take a couple of days off on the banks of Wular, and conclude the leisurely week-long trip at Baramulla.

Up there, on the bridge, it was so cold that staying a minute longer was impossible. I spotted a masala-*wallah*. Masala is a unique Kashmiri street-food item. Soft bread wrapped around chickpeas laced with a spicy chutney. I polished it off as I reached my destination, St Joseph's Church. St Joseph's school and hospital, two institutions run by missionaries of the church for hundreds of years, were the best in the area. They had also suffered casualties during the 1947 tribal raids. But I hadn't come to talk to anyone about violence, old or new. It was 24 December, and I was here to celebrate Christmas Eve.

As I stood outside the church, beside a cheerful-looking Santa Claus figure, a woman approached me. 'Excuse me, who are you?' she asked. It naturally made a lot of sense to be watchful around these parts. I told her that I was writing a travelogue. I had met the vice principal of their school two days earlier and sought permission to join in the Christmas Eve celebrations. I couldn't say for sure how much my answer had satisfied her because just then a man, who looked like a local and was presumably an employee there, arrived with some sweets and extended his best wishes to the nun. She asked him to stay a while but he was in a hurry. She offered to take him on a quick tour of the church. 'You also,' she said to me with unquestionable authority, 'you also come along. We'll all pray.'

We first gazed at the life-sized figure of Santa Claus. One of his arms was extended in an invitation for embrace. The other one rested on a stick. Next to him was a tree with strings of decorative, colourful lights. From the canopy above the church door were hung several loops of the same decorative lights. High above the church was a neon-lit Star of David. It was a small church built mostly of stone and brick.

'You know the story of Santa Claus comes from St Nicholas actually. There was once a poor man who was very worried about how to marry off his three daughters. He was very distressed. St Nicholas arrived at his doorstep and quietly dropped off three bags of gold. That's how Santa Claus, the quiet, silent beneficiary, came into existence. So every Christmas Eve we invite him to come to us again and shower us with gifts,' she explained.

We took a step sideways to admire the Christmas tree. 'This tree symbolizes the cross where Jesus died and also his birth. In Rome I have seen bread becoming flesh. When the priest prays over it, holy wine becomes blood. Jesus Christ comes alive in the mass. Come,' she said in a staccato burst and asked us to step into the church. We took our shoes off and went in.

Despite four *bukharis*—the large wood-burning stoves that are Kashmir's traditional heaters—the church was as cold within as it was outside. And the outside was very cold. These were the days of Chillai Kalan, the harshest forty-day period in Kashmir when even piped water freezes and all water, including the Dal, turns to ice. But it was extra cold this season. 'It mostly snows by this time and the temperature improves. But this time it hasn't snowed, so it is much colder this time,' the watchman outside the church had told me.

Next to the pulpit, the parishioners had built a beautiful mini-sized manger, complete with snow and colourful lights, small plants and dry twigs, in the backdrop of a blue satin-like material. From the ceiling were hung cut-outs of various letters in different languages. Colourful lights made these letters glow brilliantly. Right in front of us, the pulpit was decorated with lights and colourful fabric, and in bold white three words were inscribed on it: 'WORD MADE FLESH'. To our left were placed a keyboard, guitar and drums. The sister walked right towards the manger and said, 'See, these are letters from different languages—English, Tamil, Malayalam, Hindi, Urdu, Gurmukhi—which teach us the oneness and love there is in all our cultures. Come, let us bow our heads and pray,' she said. I quietly tiptoed my way back, leaving the two of them.

Behind the pulpit was the image of Jesus on the cross. Placed beside it were two figurines, of Joseph holding baby Jesus and Mary. Mary stood slightly taller than her husband. Above us were carved arches of wood. Although the church was carpeted quite comfortably, it was still getting colder by the second. The other two walked back to the door of the church as soon as they finished their prayers. The man offered some more gifts and sought her permission to leave. I couldn't believe I had come empty-handed.

'So,' she said, looking at me. 'What do you plan to do until the service starts?'

'I'll just sit around this place and wait, Sister,' I said.

'I'm a senior doctor at this facility,' she said sternly.

'I'm sorry. I'll just sit around this place and wait, Sister Doctor?' She inspected the church with a quick glance and left.

Nothing else happened for a while, until a sister came in and played some bars on the keyboard, checked the sound system and left. Slowly, some people started trickling in. Around 7.30 p.m., the service started with the arrival of the school's vice principal, Father John Paul.

We started with the hymn 'O Come Let Us Adore Him'. To my right, a man was praying with great solemnity, while his children danced and played around him. Everyone had moved close to the four bukharis, like iron filings around magnets, except him. He seemed indifferent to everything except devotion.

After singing a few hymns in English, the choir switched to Hindustani, beginning with 'Gloria': *Swargiya Sena aa rahi/ Meethe gaane gaa rahi/ Parvat maala bhi magan/ Ye stuti gaan gaa rahi . . .*' Nestled in a corner of north Kashmir, we must have been the most chaste Hindustani speakers for many miles around.

At around 9 p.m., the music and singing ceased as Father Paul walked up to the stage. I was sitting at an awkward angle, with my head facing the pulpit but my torso twisted towards the bukhari on which I was now resting my feet, trying to soak in some warmth. The feet were so cold, it felt like they were on fire. Father Paul thanked everyone who had come, those who had created such a beautiful manger, and wished everyone a merry Christmas before asking, 'What is Christmas?'

After a long pause, someone said it was the day when the promise of God was fulfilled.

'Christmas is the starting point of our salvation. It is an attempt to make our mortal existence immortal. Now let me ask you another question: Why did the God send his own son? Why? He was all-powerful. He could have delivered us from evil without sending his son, sitting as he was on the throne in heaven. So why did he do it?'

The cold was really climbing up the spine now. I only hoped someone among us had the correct answers.

'Okay. Let me ask another question. If an ant drops into, say, the Jhelum, and it is to be saved, tell me, how will you save it?'

No one said anything.

'See, if we jump into the Jhelum to save the ant, all the splashing will drown the ant, won't it? So who can save the ant? Only an ant can save an ant, isn't it?'

Everyone agreed. We all got the point.

With a few more hymns the service came to an end. Outside the church, at a distance from the Santa Claus, a small bonfire had been set up. Everyone gathered around it. Songs were sung, the guitar player strummed along, cakes were passed, but I couldn't hang around any longer. I greeted everyone a merry Christmas and rushed towards the home of an acquaintance in town.

I woke up the next morning with aching bones and frozen joints. But one had reasons to keep the chin up. It was Christmas! We were to assemble at the church at 10 a.m. I had about half an hour to get ready.

As soon as I walked into the church I saw a glum cameraman, of a local news channel perhaps, completely unaffected by the exuberance around him. Except for the two of us, everyone was wearing new clothes. The solemn Christian man, with a drooping moustache and thick beard, was also there, along with his son. Both were looking handsome in their indigo jackets. His daughter was wearing a beautiful red frock. Some local Muslim men and women had also come to the church, also in new clothes, which I felt was a very sincere, heart-warming gesture. A boy was called to read Isaiah 52:7:

> How beautiful on the mountains
> are the feet of those who bring good news,

who proclaim peace,
who bring good tidings,
who proclaim salvation,
who say to Zion,
'Your God reigns!'

One by one, several children stepped forward to read passages from the Bible with moving intensity. They read verses of the old making way for the new, darkness making way for light, of justice and kindness, of joy and glory. The vivid passages, given our humble circumstances and the freezing cold, brought us closer to the spirit of the event.

I remember quite distinctly the piece of writing that introduced me to the literary genius of the Bible. It was George Orwell's 'Politics and the English Language'.[2] To give an example of what a powerfully compressed and rhythmically tuned sentence sounds like, he chose this bit from Ecclesiastes:

I returned and saw under the sun, that the race is not to the swift, nor the battle to the strong, neither yet bread to the wise, nor yet riches to men of understanding, nor yet favour to men of skill; but time and chance happeneth to them all.

And then he went on to supply a parody of it in 'modern English'.

Objective considerations of contemporary phenomena compel the conclusion that success or failure in competitive activities exhibits no tendency to be commensurate with innate capacity, but that a considerable element of the unpredictable must invariably be taken into account.

It was only fitting that at the thinly attended funeral service of Orwell, an unbeliever, his friend Anthony Powell, chose to read the closing verses of Ecclesiastes:

Also when they shall be afraid of that which is high, and fears shall be in the way, and the almond tree shall flourish, and the grasshopper shall be a burden, and desire shall fail: because man goeth to his long home, and the mourners go about the streets:

Or ever the silver cord be loosed, or the golden bowl be broken, or the pitcher be broken at the fountain, or the wheel broken at the cistern/ Then shall the dust return to the earth as it was: and the spirit shall return unto God who gave it.

By around 12 p.m., the service was coming to a close. Father John Paul went up to the pulpit again. After reading a few verses, he turned towards the audience and asked, 'What is Christmas?'

Hadn't we settled this yesterday?

'Tree decorations, Santa Claus, are these things in themselves enough? No, they aren't. St Augustine stressed the importance of God becoming human. That is the spirit of Christmas. Also, Christmas signifies,' Father Paul went on to state, 'God's love, God's gift, God's Power and God's Sacrifice', explaining each point in detail. He had the calm, soothing lilt of a radio announcer. Father Paul thanked everyone, including the non-Christians who had come to share their happiness, and church members who had pitched in to make the day worth remembering. By around 12.15 p.m., we were out in the sun, having tea, eating cake.

I asked the father where he had come from and how he had ended up in such a distant place. 'I was in Akhnoor [Jammu] before this. There were around 220 Catholic families there. Back then, on Christmas Eve, you would have seen so many young boys and girls working together to decorate the church and all. It used to be a different atmosphere there. There are no Christian families here outside the staff quarters of the school and hospital in this compound. Even in Srinagar you'll find twenty, twenty-two families.

'I was nineteen years old when I joined the diocese of Jammu and Srinagar. I've been serving in this region for the past eighteen, nineteen years now. These are really old and important institutions. That building you see over there, it is part of our school and it's over 120 years old.'

Given the harsh winters, the restrictions and all, did he consider his stint here as what in administrative circles is referred to as a 'punishment posting'?

He laughed and said, 'I'm new here but with these tight conditions . . . they make life slightly dull. As in, after you're done with your duties at the institutions you have few colleagues to go to, to spend time with. Back in Akhnoor you had a church every few kilometres. Up here it's slightly difficult. Otherwise there's not much to complain about.'

Except the lack of good plum cake?

'Haha. Yeah, there's that.'

I wished him a merry Christmas and was preparing to leave when I felt a tap on my shoulder. It was Sister Doctor! She had brought me a box of sweets. But how could I, who was already wilting in shame for not bringing any gifts or sweets, possibly accept it? She could give the sweets instead to the visitors who were still pouring into the church. 'You came all the way, son. It's yours. Merry Christmas,' she said with a smile.

3

The Winds of Sopore

I asked Afzal Sofi to take me through the conversation he had had with the organizers of Sundance Film Festival one more time. 'They called and said that our movie had won some award. They said, "We are sending you the tickets. You have to come here immediately."'

And he told them what?

'I'm not lying. I told them I can't come. I was too lazy to go. And really, I didn't know about Sundance. I made some silly excuse about the weather being bad or something. It was much later that my friends told me what a big deal Sundance is.'

In 2012, *Valley of Saints*, the feature film in which Sofi played the supporting role, won the World Cinema Dramatic Audience Award and the Alfred P. Sloan Feature Film Prize at the Sundance film festival, which is hosted every year at the Sundance Institute in Utah, US. The film, which also won the special jury prize at Dubai Film Festival, was praised by movie critics at the *New York Times*, *Village Voice*, Indiewire, Hollywood Reporter, Variety and RogerEbert.com. It still remains the most critically acclaimed feature film that deals with, and is set in, Kashmir.

It's a story about two close friends—the boatman Gulzar (played by real-life boatman Gulzar) and Afzal (played by Afzal)—who are trying to escape Kashmir to start their lives afresh. But before they can leave, a strict curfew is enforced, confining them to their home in the Dal. There they come across, by chance, an American-Kashmiri researcher, Asifa (played by Neelofar Hamid), who's doing a study on the pollution in the lake. Romance brews between Gulzar and Asifa as he shows her around the Dal. Afzal gets jealous of Gulzar and their friendship is threatened.

'Nobody imagined that the film would do so well. After its release, things got slightly crazy. We went to Germany [*Valley of Saints* also opened the 2012 Hamburg International Film Festival], we went to Dubai, our movie was shown at Rotterdam as well.

'I remember perfect strangers approaching Gulzar and me for autographs. When it happened for the first time, I went up to Musa [Musa Syeed, the writer/director] and asked him, "What do people write in autographs?" He said, "Just sign your name." We were completely out of our depths. We would run away from interviews and reporters would complain that we were playing hard to get. *Us waqt lagta tha hum bhi kuch hain* [It felt like we had arrived].

'It was a nerve-wracking experience the first time Gulzar and I travelled outside India. There was this Russian city in which we landed where a female inspector shouted at me. I don't know whether it was my appearance or my name. I felt humiliated. This happens to me still. They shout in my face. And ask me, "Why do you have blue eyes? Where are you from really?" In my heart I've made peace with it . . . *Jab safar lamba hota hai, kaafi cheezein samajh aati hain* [When the journey is long, we learn a lot of things]. We met a lot of actors and directors at these film festivals and exchanged notes with them.

'I wasn't meant to play the supporting role to begin with. My job initially was with Musa to find actors and, once we had zeroed in on Gulzar, to work with our lead on his acting. But Musa thought our chemistry worked well and cast me in the movie. It was a great experience. Even while returning from a festival, at Srinagar airport, an American lady recognized us and asked for our autographs. I couldn't believe our film had been watched so widely.'

Sofi has a really good scene in the movie. It's a new dawn, full of possibilities, and Gulzar wants to make the most of it with his friend but Afzal doesn't want to get up. To amuse his friend, and to buy some more time in bed, Afzal does a little act—how people look in their deaths.

He begins by showing what natural deaths look like. Afzal lies straight on his back, expressionless, with his arms placed over his chest, like a person in deep sleep. Then he shows us what sudden deaths look like. His posture doesn't change much, except there is a crazed look on his face which is now slightly bent to one side. Then he does a mime of people who've died violent deaths. He contorts his body, bends his limbs at unnatural angles, and lifts his shirt to show some flesh around his waist. Gulzar gets intrigued and asks his friend to enact his own corpse. Afzal does a dead body with a happy face. To show Gulzar's corpse, he does a dead body with a sad face. The two have a good laugh and walk out of the frame, leaving behind a temporary emptiness.

As the euphoria over the movie ebbed, Sofi returned to his studies. In 2013, he finished his MPhil from Kashmir University and tried to get into journalism. Why did he not continue working in movies?

'I don't know. It didn't really work out for me after the success of *Valley of Saints*. I went for some auditions but nothing happened. There were some projects I wanted to do but for some reason or the other they fizzled out.'

Sofi worked as a journalist for a few weeks after getting his master's but the salary was unsustainably low. He moved on to work in the social sector, and during the following year, in 2014, when floods struck the valley, he did advocacy work on behalf of ActionAid, an NGO. He worked with another group documenting cases of torture and disappearances. A year later, he got an opportunity of the sort he had been waiting for. He was asked to start and manage a media studies department in Baramulla's Government Degree College.

'There was nobody to teach Kashmiri kids the basics of making films, of handling a camera, editing, etc. I practically built that department from scratch. My students and I have already made around five films, which we've sent to various film festivals. We're making more.'

But the restrictions on communication after 5 August 2019 have made life tough for him and his students. His contract with the college was to be renewed just before 5 August, but administrative activities came to a halt after the lockdown. The academic work also got affected because there was no Internet. 'So these days I'm not doing much, except sitting at my uncle's shop and selling undergarments,' he said.

Afzal and I were talking in a car which he was directing around the streets of Sopore showing me places of interest. There was the shop where he sat all day, there was the market that had been burnt down several times, and those were the places where he had spent his childhood. We were moving along the Jhelum in Old Sopore town when Afzal grew quiet. 'We used to live in this area long back,' he said after a few moments of silence. I asked him about his childhood.

'I was seven or eight years old in 1989. I have some memories of the conflict. Militants used to be everywhere. Non-Kashmiris had also come bearing arms. Then counter-insurgency operations picked up. Informers were everywhere. Guns were everywhere. But the clearest memory I have is from a day in 1993. I remember every second of it.

'Earlier that day, some militants had snatched rifles from paramilitary soldiers not far from here. The soldiers were furious.

They fired upon a vehicle they saw coming towards this area. Maybe they thought it was full of militants. Employees of the handloom department were returning from their day's work. All of them died. One of them was my father. A mute neighbour of ours had seen the entire episode. He came running towards our house and gesticulated. We understood what he was trying to say. But another neighbour who had just returned from Srinagar said she had spotted my father somewhere there. The mute gesticulated expressing outrage. He had seen my father's bullet-riddled body. Then someone spotted bodies in shrouds being brought towards our colony. I saw my father's body. I embraced him and shrieked. I still remember that unnatural shriek.'[1]

How did it affect his life afterwards?

'I wanted to grow up quickly and become a militant. For a long time, because of him, the regular crackdowns, daily harassment, I could think of nothing else. I still have a recurring nightmare—I'm running towards my home with a gun in my hands while soldiers are chasing me. I reach my house but am scared because I can't find a place to hide my gun . . . You know, conflict is like a gust of wind. It can blow you, like a straw, in any direction. It can make you do anything.

'Eventually I found peace through my religion. Faith gave me stillness and peace. After finding that peace, I have been looking back at my life, at my decisions, at my beliefs.'

For Afzal, religion came as an antidote to violence and the trauma it left behind. 'People find solace in different things. There are also people who have bottomed out so thoroughly that it is hard for them to emerge at all. When I used to work for an NGO on mental health issues, to give you an example, I met one such person while we were conducting a door-to-door exercise. She was an old woman who couldn't stop crying. The entire day she held the photo of her son to her chest and wept. That's all she had been doing for several years. As happened to so many other families here, her son just disappeared one day. I said to her, "Take all this pain in your heart and crush it under your feet. It will all go away and you'll feel lighter." The lady started weeping even harder. When I asked her why, she replied, "How can you ask me to crush the memories of my son?"

'We set up a small shop for her outside her house. People who came to buy groceries would also hang around and chat with her. Slowly, through these regular conversations, her condition improved. But she would still ask me in our occasional meetings, "Could you somehow get him in my dreams? The nights when I don't see him, I feel quite wretched." Interactions like these changed me a lot. They helped me deal with my own pain. I used to break down often, thinking about my father. I still do, in fact, but I think I have a better control over my emotions now.'

If conflict, as he says, is like a gust of wind, then he's a straw that has been caught in a crossfire of winds which have hauled him up towards the stars and brought him down to the ground. But he's content with how far he has come. 'Some of my students, with whom I'm making films, are unbelievably talented. We've made a lot of progress . . . I suppose we can't go back from here, can we?'

SRINAGAR

1

A Walk along the Bund

One of the best things to do in Srinagar, in any season, is to take a walk on the Bund, along the Jhelum, between Zero Bridge and Amira Kadal. It is the only stretch around the city centre where you can walk at any time of the day, or night, uninterrupted by noise or people. One could start from Zero Bridge, which looks good in the evenings when its intricately designed wooden panels, lit with artificial light, casts patterns on the flowing water below. Away from the clamour of the Dal and other tourist spots, this narrow walkway is tucked behind some of the oldest shops in the city.

One of them is an old cafe called Hotel Lala Sheikh, whose bleak Dostoevskian cavern shields its occupants from street noise and mobile networks. Close by is an over-hundred-year-old photo studio, the Mahatta, which possesses some rare, vintage photos of the valley, and a famous handicraft store, Suffering Moses, which was founded in 1840. Opposite them is a small park with an elegant mosque, and in its courtyard one can find people of all ages, from toddlers to old men, hanging around, chatting or playing cricket till sundown.

A little further ahead you come to the Abi Guzar area. Here once stood a building, set up by the Dogra rulers in the nineteenth century, through which tax was collected from boats bringing goods into Srinagar. This was the time when, in the absence of reliable road transport, goods were shipped on the river. The building's now gone, though the name remains.

A few hundred metres down is a peaceful Christian graveyard shaded by a huge Chinar tree. Adjoining it, towards the Bund, is a smaller Muslim graveyard. In this even quieter part of the Bund, young people can often be spotted walking around holding hands or sitting by the banks. It is said that British officers, during their holidays, preferred staying around the Bund. Some of the earliest houseboats of the valley were anchored in this area, to be their summer retreats.

From here the arch of Amira Kadal (*kadal* means bridge in Kashmiri) becomes visible. On most days it is bustling with vendors selling cheap cutlery, denims, fish, handy electronic items, and more. Amira Kadal marks the end of the Bund. And this is usually from where I return. But on this day in late 2019, I travelled further, on a more personal journey.

Over the bridge to the right is an old Hanuman temple, barricaded by soldiers at all times. This is where my parents met for the first time. A soldier at the entrance asks for my identity. 'We used to live here,' I say. 'Oh, they are the '90 *wallah* party,' he says to his colleague, referring to the year when Pandits left the valley. There is a small basin inside which these words are etched: 'Constructed by/ Lt Col DR Puri/ In ever-loving memory/ of his wife/ Krishna/ who departed on/ 4th March 1962'.

A five-minute walk later, I reach Lal Ded Hospital. Somewhere in its maternity ward I was born.

Our locality wasn't much developed in those days. But one could get the essentials from Lal Mandi which was very near.

I had spoken to an uncle about our life in Srinagar, and snatches of his description came to mind as I walked on this road again. From here, it takes around twenty minutes to reach what once was our home. In over a decade of travelling to Kashmir on reporting assignments, I had never gone there. I was too young when we left Kashmir. Too young to remember my way back. I had tried finding the house once, through the images my parents had built in my mind of our neighbourhood, through the bundle of photographs we had managed to salvage before leaving. I clearly remember one photograph in which I'm sitting on my uncle's bright red Yezdi motorcycle.

You remember the motorcycle? You used to sit on the tank, hold the handles and make growling noises.

I walked right into our locality, called up my father, and told him I was there. He tried explaining the location to me. In the background I could hear my parents arguing over the best way to reach our house, the landmarks, the neighbours' houses.

'Now there on the left, do you see it?' my father asked. I was standing in front of it. I had returned after more than a decade. We had come here in 2007, my parents and I, on a road trip from Jammu for the first time after our exodus. I was standing right where we had stood twelve years ago. Not even a minute had passed before we left because my parents were still quite scared, of something, a stray bullet, 'who knows?' And just like that we turned back. Less than a minute is what a family got to look at the house that was once exclusively its own.

'What do you hear?' my father asked. I heard noises. I told him so. There was a silence. 'Click a photograph but don't stay there too long,' my mother said. She asked if anything had changed. The entrance had been shifted to another location, I told her. The front doors were open.

Rahul Pandita in *Our Moon Has Blood Clots*[1] has a passage about him returning to the home that his family had sold after their exile. When he rings the bell to the house where he grew up, which was once his own, what does Pandita say to the present owner? Nothing. It is a friend of his who ends up saying, 'Actually, he used to live here long ago.' Pandita, who couldn't even knock on the doors to that house, then stepped in. I couldn't do that. I can't imagine having a conversation with the people who own our house now. What do we even talk about?

Back at our house in Delhi we talk about what our home was like. I mostly listen. This time I went back to my uncle and listened till I got it all down—a short story about another sort of journey, the one away from home.

We used to live in a place called Munshi mohalla in Ali Kadal, downtown Srinagar. In 1965 your grandfather, 'Tathaji', bought some land very far away from Shahar. As years passed, the city expanded and our house came to be in its very centre. We added floors on floors, over time, to that house till we had three. Each floor had four rooms, a bath and kitchen.

In those days, we used to eat on chowkis—raised wooden planks—in the main kitchen. The elders used to eat on bigger chowkis. We had smaller, wobbly chowkis and curries in our thalis were always running away. In Delhi people carry their lunch to their offices. In our house, everyone had to have their lunch before leaving for work. One poor uncle who worked far away in Chadoora had to have his at 6.30 in the morning.

We lived a leisurely life. Schools started at 10 in summers, at 11 in winters. But Tathaji's mother, Mataji, enforced strict discipline in the house. Dinner could not be skipped. Discipline also was followed in the rationing of everyday items like coal, kerosene, rice.

Our locality wasn't very developed in those days. But one could get the essentials from Lal Mandi which was very near. Sri Pratap library was close by, as was Amar Singh college. Within one kilometre was Lal Ded hospital where you were born. Three well-stocked pharmacies were also within walking distance. Not far from us were also two wine shops. One was near Lal Ded hospital, the other near Lal Mandi.

We used to have some very fine doctors then. There was this legendary physician, Dr Ali Jaan. There was Dr D.N. Thussu and Dr Puran Raina.

You remember the motorcycle in our house? You used to sit on the tank, hold the handles and make growling noises. Once you fell from it, grievously injuring the motorcycle.

Culture was treasured in our house and music was shared. We were great fans of K.L. Saigal and Begum Akhtar. I would not miss a single music concert. I heard Bhimsen Joshi in Nishat Bagh from a distance of 10 metres once. He was right in front of me. There was a power outage while he was singing, but it did not affect him, he continued singing, and by the flowing waters of the garden, in the stillness of the evening, it felt like paradise. I attended a Dagar brothers' concert in Pari Mahal, drove all the way, some 90 kilometres, on my motorcycle, to attend a performance in Pahalgam.

Kishori Amonkar had come to Gulmarg for a concert. But it had rained, so the proceedings had been shifted indoors. There, in the middle of her performance, a politician notorious for his wayward behaviour was chastised by Amonkar for slanting on a sofa and chewing paan during her concert. 'Yahan gaana ho raha hai, koi mujra nahi ho raha,' she had said. Like a scared little schoolboy, he sat in attention for the rest of the night.

And then it started, in '86. Our temples were set on fire one after another. Some Hindu leaders had told us not to worry. 'If anything happens, the entire country will stand up with you.' Nobody stood up. Nothing happened. The temples continued to be burnt. Violence had begun to unfold. In '87 we saw guns for the first time. In '88 we heard about killings. In '89 we felt death approaching us. They killed Tika Lal Taploo. But one could still delude oneself. One could still think they wouldn't come for us. But when we heard about what they did to Sarla Bhatt [a nurse who was abducted and gangraped before being killed] *. . . It shook us to the core. We knew then that it had ended. What had she done? How could we live in a place like that? In a place where even a scholar like Sarwanand Kaul Premi* *was not spared? Days passed like that and nobody stood up for us. Papers in Urdu kept writing threatening letters to us.*

On the night of 19 January 1990, we were watching a movie on TV when suddenly, around 10.30, megaphones sounded everywhere. 'Get out of your house,' the voices commanded. There was a sense of finality in those voices. We climbed up to the third floor with some heavy stones in our hands, sure that those were our last hours. We thought we would at least take down one or two of them before they killed us. We were still shaking when dawn broke. Not one friend, not one acquaintance with whom we had shared our lives, came to check on us that night. Or any other night after that. All of them vanished.

After some three weeks was Shivratri. For us this night used to mean family gatherings, lots of food, elders telling us stories about the marriage of Shiv and Parvati; all our happy memories were woven around this night. Walnuts used to be exchanged between families, especially between families of recently married couples. This night Tathaji was chanting the mantras almost inaudibly. When the time came and I began to blow the conch, he slapped me across the face. 'Do you want to kill us?'

After fifteen days, we had to leave. Your mother and father had taken you to Delhi, and just then you had suffered a fracture. We left with two pairs of clothes each. We couldn't be seen moving out with all our belongings openly. They used to say, 'Kya sa Hangul ma goi nazri [You wouldn't happen to have seen any Kashmiri stags, would you]?' Because we had become a rare species like Hangul.

Mataji never understood what had happened. She would ask us to go out and fetch some tea, some sugar, rice, as if we were still in Kashmir. She remained disoriented till her death. The poor woman did not know how to communicate with her Delhi neighbours so she used to gesticulate to them. Sometimes it worked. She went out once herself to buy something and didn't return until evening when she was brought by two kind men. 'You would have probably never found her. She kept saying I live in the big house,' one of the two men said. We had found a small place in an unauthorized colony in the trans-Yamuna area. The power supply used to be erratic, water could only be fetched through an old hand pump. There were two rooms, and a couple was living in one. The landlord asked us for Rs 10,000 so that with our advance rent he could make us an extra room. We gave him the last penny we had. Tathaji had retired by then and none of us, except your father, had a job. It took a long time for us to be able to afford a cooler.

Having no money, no jobs meant that we had a lot of free time. We spent it as volunteers at the Kashmiri Samiti office in Lajpat Nagar. Every day we saw [new] families come. Some of them were clothed in tatters. All we could do was give them some food, water and a temporary roof over their heads. Some hadn't eaten in many days. Some had lost their family members. Every family was given a 6x6 carpet space and some utensils. Imagine a family living like that. Many fell ill here. We heard of the people back in Jammu. They were dying of snakebites and heat. Our women were the worst hit. Our sense of privacy and dignity received daily blows.

It was in one such moment of desperation that we decided to march up to Prime Minister V.P. Singh's residence. From Chandni Chowk, we started for his house. Many of us did not know how to protest, we were doing this for the first time in our lives. We were stopped right outside his house and not let in. When we continued to march, in defiance, policemen threw us into buses and took us to Mandir Marg police station. We spent that evening in the lock-up. You must understand our situation then. As I told you we were really desperate then. With nothing else to do, to divert our attention from our hungry bellies, the 300 of us started singing our bhajan 'Maej Sharikeay kar daya var dayai bhaweni'.

But those episodes also broke a lot of class barriers. We were an intensely class-conscious society. We looked down upon our bakers, for instance. But these adversities broke all those prejudices. There was a baker, Kanhaiya Lal Kandur. We used to call him

Kani Kandur. He was a huge man. At our samiti in Lajpat Nagar, he took charge of our security. We looked up to him, with pride.

We went for many demonstrations and hunger strikes. It was incredible that till much later people did not even know what had happened to us. When I joined my office, some of my colleagues would smirk at me. They couldn't understand how we couldn't bear the heat of the plains, why on one summer day I asked for a glass of water and instead of drinking it, poured it on my head.

We didn't get much time to get our belongings from our house. We went there in November '90. Minutes after we entered our house our neighbours said, 'Leave quickly or they will kill you.' I had less than an hour and several lifetimes of belongings. What one thing could I have picked over other? I was reaching out for a bag when a bundle of rope fell down, scraping me on my back. I raised my arms in surrender. Only after many seconds passed and nothing happened did I realize what had happened. None of us ever went there again. Tathaji wrote letters to the prime minister and the president when we were told that people had broken into our house. I went to see our house after twenty years, I remember how it felt. Like an asthmatic I would take deep breaths throughout that trip to Kashmir, trying to soak in as much air as I could of my homeland.

Till now I don't know why we were thrown out. Why were we targeted? Had we harmed any of them? Did we not, under threat, follow them to their political rallies? Then what was our fault? To those who say that we left because of state conspiracy, tell them our story.

2

Sitting by the Jhelum

Of all the Kashmiris I spoke with, I revisited two people to understand how their lives and the lives of those around them had changed after the abrogation of Article 370. These two had nothing in common except that I had first met them at the Bund. They came from very different backgrounds and worked in different professions where they dealt with their own sets of challenges.

Dr Aijaz Ahmad Bund is an assistant professor at the Government Degree College for Women, Pulwama. He is also the founder of the Sonzal Welfare Trust in Srinagar, which perhaps is the only organization of its kind working for the rights of the LGBTQ+ community in the valley. In 2018, he wrote a book called *The Hijras of Kashmir: A Marginalized Form of Personhood.*[1] It sparked, for the first time in Kashmir, a debate on the status of the LGBTQ+ community, which he describes in his book as an 'ethnic minority'. We first spoke to each other a few days before 5 August 2019. Dr Aijaz, who was well-mannered and courteous to a fault, came dressed in a simple shirt and trousers, wearing a working-class look.

'It was in 2008 when a transgender woman came to our house with a marriage proposal for my sister. For the longest time my mother wouldn't allow her inside the home but relented after I intervened. But after the transwoman left, I saw my mother washing the cups that our guest had used, not once, not twice, but thrice. As if the visitor had polluted something very deep inside our house. I was very disturbed by that incident,' Dr Aijaz said.

In 2011 he started discussing the subject in his classroom, at Kashmir University's MA, social work class. He was ridiculed and harassed by his peers. 'Nobody was ready to hear what I had to say. It's in those classrooms that I started my fight, that my life changed.'

He fought hard to get people to listen to the marginalized voices and to create temporary safe spaces for people from the community. And he did these things in a place as volatile and violent as Kashmir.

'One feels a sort of toxic masculinity at work here. Sometimes the resistance here takes hyper-masculine overtones. I think men feel threatened that their patriarchal structures will come crumbling down if they allow sexual freedom to minorities. Women don't feel as threatened. It is difficult to hold a discussion about sexual rights in Kashmir. Elsewhere you don't find such difficulties. You can have pride marches in Delhi. Not here.'

People who don't fit into conventional social categories are told that the only issue to bother with is the conflict. Dr Aijaz feels deeply about this. This, he argued, was a way to crush the independent identities of sexual minorities. To indefinitely put off a matter that needed to be addressed urgently. 'How can the rights of the community be sidelined? Our issues will remain. We will remain where we are, no matter which way the political winds blow. If religion doesn't recognize us, if the state doesn't recognize us, where do we go? What do we do with "Azadi" in which even our existence is not acknowledged?'

Dr Aijaz worked for years to get people to confront their prejudices. But a lot of what he achieved was undone after the government imposed a curfew, cut off telephone lines and banned the Internet across the valley from 5 August 2019.

'There were people who did not know for as long as six months whether their partners were dead or alive. So many people described to me later how cathartic the experience was of hearing the first "hello" from their partners on the phone. They wept and wept. It was a very difficult time for all of us. People who were connected to each other and to the global LGBTQ+ community through the Internet suddenly found themselves alone and disoriented,' Dr Aijaz said.

Dr Aijaz and his team were running several mental health programmes for the community. It all came to an abrupt halt after 5 August 2019. The safe spaces that he had worked so hard to create vanished.

But the most severe trauma was faced by those who were forced, because of the curfew, to live with their abusers 24x7. 'When schools and colleges were open, many were able to avoid their abusers, at least temporarily. During that time of absolute confinement, lots of people reported domestic violence and abuse. Then, there were people taking hormones; with the markets suddenly shut, many developed gender dysphoria and developed severe suicidal thoughts,' he said.

Many people from the community have still not been able to see each other in person because restrictions from 5 August 2019 have dovetailed into the restrictions placed on the meeting of people after the outbreak of COVID-19.

Religion has been a coping mechanism for many in the community. In *Hijras of Kashmir*, Aijaz discusses how religion is a vital element in the lives of LGBTQ+ community members in Kashmir. For many, it is the only accessible form of therapy, the only source of solace.

And faith also, surely, gives its adherents the right to protest, to lodge a complaint against their maker? In the same book he quotes a person who expresses his deep anguish in these words:

I am the one who is living the absolute torment of occupying a body that is never coordinated with who I am inside. It is never easy to accept what I am? Am I a man? A woman or what? But I am sure that I am a human being, I see, feel and react. I have emotions. *Agar khodayan mard te zanaaneh yaetchie banawih telih kaem banaiew aiess. Soun aasun agar galti chi telih chi so khodai senz galti. Sanih aasnuk kus chu kosoorwar kraal ha kinih baaneh, banawan woul ha kinih bandeh?*

[If God created only men and women then who created us? If we are mistakes then undoubtedly we are God's mistakes. For my existence who is to blame, potter, or the pot; creator or the creation?]

The thing that really got under Dr Aijaz's skin, he said, was the hypocrisy of his society. He gives the example of a transgender person who lives in downtown Srinagar. The person, he says, used to be quite active in protests against the administration, and attained a heroic status among some locals. But ironically, the sexual identity of that person still wasn't accepted. There are doors that remain closed to her. There are prejudices even her bravado hasn't been able to break.

'How do I explain it to you . . . It's like there are some people who live among you, who do everything they can for you, and you still look right through them. As if they don't even exist,' Dr Aijaz said.

Sometimes, it feels to him as if he's swimming across a double current, blindly flapping his exhausted limbs in order to survive, 'and at the end of it you find yourself still at the starting point, not having covered any distance. There is politics within the community and there's oppression outside it. *Kis kis se ladein, ab utni zindagi bhi nahi hai* [whom all do we fight, we don't even have that much time left on earth]?'

Dr Aijaz may occasionally sound despondent and angry, but he also exudes the warmth of a leisurely bonfire. No wonder the stories he told me when we met at the Bund before 5 August felt so believable: Of how strangers from across the valley called him in extreme distress, and how his presence usually had a calming effect not just on the survivors but on the families as well, who in most cases turned out to be the perpetrators of violence. I had nothing more to ask. But I did express my admiration for his work. Dr Aijaz smiled at the compliment and wished me luck.

~

In journalist Quratulain Rehbar, I found the two voices that I had been looking for. The first was the voice of an articulate young Kashmiri who had observed her society closely and had written about it, often at great personal risk. The second voice was of a fiercely independent young woman. I began by asking Rehbar what took her towards journalism.

'Because I've been waiting to speak up. Women are brought up everywhere with an instruction to remain quiet. Always. Men are always apprehensive of what women will say if they're involved in the conversations. What sort of opinions will she come up with?'

Rehbar was born in 1993 at a time when crackdowns were quite common. 'Forces used to barge into our homes frequently. Even as a child with no experience of the world outside, I could sense that things were not right. Everything about that atmosphere just felt wrong. When these things happen routinely, you grow up feeling disoriented all the time.'

She was twelve when, while visiting her mother's family, she heard an armed soldier shout obscenities at her from a bunker. This was the first time she felt helpless and vulnerable. It's a memory that keeps haunting her when she steps out for work. Twelve years later, she discovered how close she, and everyone else around her, was to death.

Rehbar was in the Nowgam campus of Central University of Kashmir attending a class when she got a phone call from her best friend, who lived next door. Some militants had barged into her friend's house, and just like that her house had turned into an encounter site. Only her friend and her mother were in the house when it happened. Rehbar rushed there immediately.

That day was like a dream, Rehbar said. After two hours, the mother and her daughter were allowed to come out of the house. The house that took seven years to build was reduced to ashes over the next twelve hours. Rehbar says that such experiences made her want to pick up the pen.

At the time I met her, Rehbar was pursuing a heart-rending story. It was about a young, cheerful girl who had lived a sheltered life. 'She enjoyed wearing colourful clothes and liked studying very much. Then suddenly, her brother went missing. Some said he'd picked up the gun. The world turned upside down for her. She turned into someone else. Her elderly parents couldn't do much. They kept mourning at home. So this girl made an excuse to her parents—of having joined tuition classes—and went from village to village, door to door, wearing a burqa so that nobody could identify her, with a photo of her brother, asking people if they had seen him. This went on for months. She went on to take a job while doing this. Conflict had made her emotionally quite mature. Or maybe these aren't the right words to describe what I'm trying to say. I mean, it affects women very differently,' she said.

I had come across a similar story a few days ago. A woman whose son had died in a counter-insurgency operation in the valley, whose identity I agreed not to disclose, told me, 'When I lost my husband, routine life became difficult for me. Not having a husband makes life very tough. I can tell you what would have happened had I died instead of my husband. He would have remarried immediately. The children would have grown up better. They would have had little to worry about. But I couldn't do the same. I lived my life alone. And when my son died, they consoled me by saying you're the mother of a *Shahid* (martyr). That he had died for the cause. But now whether we get azadi or not, my world is finished. Is it not? What do I have to look forward to? Azadi is for those who are happy. Isn't it?'

Rehbar was angry about women in Kashmir being targeted for allegedly being *mukhbirs* [informers]. 'Now look at the story of this girl, what she has gone through, how she has abandoned everything to go from door to door looking for her brother. Now tell me what you think? Would you dare stick a label on all of us? Call us finicky, ignorant, untrustworthy, *mukhbir*? The conflict demands absolute perfection from everyone, every time. But guess what, nobody's perfect.'

I asked her how the nullification of Article 370 had affected her, as a young Kashmiri and as a journalist.

'I was in Srinagar when it happened. Earlier, whenever anything of this sort happened—clashes, curfew, restrictions—I would call my mother and reassure her of my safety. But this time I couldn't do that. This added to panic on both sides, I suppose. When I woke up that day, I knew something had happened. Our phones were not working, the Internet was not working. The aunty I used to live with in Srinagar's downtown area said there were a lot of armed soldiers outside our house. Somehow I managed to walk several kilometres to my office. When our boss reached office, some three or four hours later during that day, he told us what had happened. I cried. All of us at the office cried . . . I can't tell you why exactly but there was just a sudden sense of loneliness. I was carrying along the collected edition of Agha Shahid Ali's poems. With nothing to do, I sat down and started reading him. He gave me a lot of strength.'

Her recollection of the next one week following the 5 August announcement is a flurry of emotions. The first thing she remembers is her work. She worked like a robot, she says, scribbling notes and typing stories till her fingers ached. She travelled to far-flung places with another female colleague on a Scooty on deserted and barricaded roads. She remembers worrying for her brother since she had heard reports about young boys being picked up and put in jail. And she didn't get any salary for the next three months, so she sustained her work through her own savings.

'Looking back, I feel proud of myself—the way I overcame fear and reported stories whose publication I felt was a matter of life and death for me.'

Was the period after 5 August 2019 tougher for women?

Rehbar recalls statements made by mainstream Indian political leaders who said that with the abrogation of Article 370, men from the mainland 'can bring brides from Kashmir'. Women in Kashmir were very scared for their safety, she says.

'It really drove a lot of parents here mad. They wouldn't allow their daughters to step out. I have a friend who suffers from depression. She did not have access to the Internet, phone, television, anything. And her parents had forbidden her to step out of the house. She was really sinking when I met her two weeks after restrictions were enforced. After our first meeting, she requested me to keep coming back for at least one hour every day. It was a very tough time. That period still hasn't ended for a lot of us.'

I had much more to ask her but Rehbar had to rush for a story. For someone who is not even in her thirties yet, Rehbar has seen and absorbed far more than most journalists do in their lifetimes. She hopes to write a book one day. When that happens, I joked with her, we should do the interview in reverse.

3

Talking Theatre in Barzulla

Many in Kashmir know the playwright, actor and director Bashir Bhawani from his cameos in *Haider* and *Bajrangi Bhaijaan*. But what is not as widely known is the story of how a village boy from south Kashmir ended up in the finest theatre institute in India—the National School of Drama, NSD. It interested me immensely when I first heard that someone from rural south Kashmir had gone to NSD in the early eighties. How had he even got to know about it? Did he ever meet its legendary founder-director, Ebrahim Alkazi? I went to meet Bashir at his home in Barzulla to find out.

Bashir was conducting a major renovation of his house when I visited it in August 2019. After sweetly apologizing for the mess, he led me into a room where we spent the next couple of hours or so talking about theatre.

'I have a very basic question about theatre, which I put before every class that I teach. People are dying everywhere, aren't they? There aren't enough houses, basic needs of people are often never met, so why conduct theatre? I was in Guwahati some time back and I asked my class the same question,' he started off by saying.

'*Theatre kisi bhi qaum ko jeene ka tareeqa sikhata hai. Logon ko zinda rehne ka hunar theatre ne diya hai* [Theatre has taught communities how to live. It has taught people the art of living]. Look up any society, in the absence of theatre, it withers.

'It is all the more important for those of us who have been striving for our own identity to acknowledge the role of theatre in shaping our character. A character that was forged over many years with the thoughtful, collective efforts of Sikhs, Pandits and Muslims.

'*Magar hum kya karte hain? Tanz. "Yimayi Bhand"* [But what do we instead do? We scoff at them. "These street performers"] We look down upon what should otherwise be a serious, significant, sensible aspect of our society.'

He took his theory about the need for theatre further. All the civilizations that have vanished, he said, were found running away, ashamed of their own cultures. Culture and heritage are things that hold a group of people together. Those who don't preserve their culture and heritage fade away without a trace.

He said Kashmiris used to lord over a great space once. 'We Kashmiris weren't just confined between Khadanyar [north] to Khanabal [south]. We were spread from Gilgit till here and beyond.' Kashmiris, he says, were intrinsically inclined towards art and culture, which is why despite some very violent periods in their history, times when they came quite close to being finished, they survived through their writings, folk tales, customs. Bashir said it was his staunch belief that wherever a Kashmiri is, he or she is inherently disposed towards assimilating, engaging with art and culture. 'That's our only in-built survival mechanism,' he said.

At this very crucial juncture, Bashir was interrupted by the building contractor. Sandpapers, not of the type that Bashir had got earlier that day but of a different grade, were required. Also, the circular electric saw that they were working the tiles with required a new set of teeth. He went outside to deal with the matter while I, who hadn't had any breakfast that morning, wiped clean the plate of biscuits which his wife had kindly brought us some time back and which I had been eyeing for a long time.

My mouth was still stuffed with biscuits when Bashir returned. 'Have I told you how I started doing theatre?'

Hmm hmm, I said.

Bashir was born in Doru-Shahabad, which used to host an annual 'Jashn-e-Rasuul Mir'—'By the way, on the issue of Rasuul Mir can I say something? I don't know why, but we only seem to beget poets in our society. Without poets our civilization seems to not have any meaning. Why's this?'

The Jashn-e-Rasuul Mir was a big festival where artists from across the valley would come to celebrate his poetry. Bashir first got on to the stage in one of those events. Gandhi Jayanti was another such occasion. Schools would be asked to do little skits. 'It was in one of those Gandhi events that I did my first proper role on stage. I played the role of a father, and I still remember my first dialogue: "*Bapu sund doh chu, ayis gasav manaavne*" [It is Bapu's day. We'll go to commemorate]. This was in October 1962.'

So he had been in professional theatre for fifty-seven years now. But theatre wasn't his first choice. He got into painting and sculpting. It was in his Anantnag college that he was first introduced to theatre by one of his professors, Rattan Lal Shah. Shah was the head of their dramatic society. After college, Bashir started working on theatre with boys from around south Kashmir's villages. He said he had an ambition to make something out of them. The theatre scene was meanwhile growing strong. He got to work with a lot of talented people like Ali Mohammad Lone and Chaman Lal Chaman. Together, they started a parallel 'Yaum-e-Rasuul Mir' annual event. The conventional festival had started losing lustre.

'It was Mr Rattan Lal Shah who asked me once, "Why don't you go to NSD?" I did not know what it was. I asked him. By then I had won all the state awards [theatre]. He said NSD was the best school to learn theatre from and that's where I needed to be.' So Bashir sent NSD a letter. This was in 1982. They said that the admission session was over for that year. He applied again the following year. Again he missed the deadline by a week. They asked him to send his application again, but this time before March. 'Then my mother said that she wouldn't allow me to go outside Kashmir unless I got married. So I married and carried on with my theatre activities, waiting to apply to NSD,' Bashir said.

Meanwhile, people in his circle had got to know that he was trying hard to get into the prestigious theatre school. 'One of them made a remark about how a Kashmiri Muslim from a village could not get into NSD even in his dreams. That was it for me. I promised myself that if I did not get through to NSD, in what would then be my last attempt since I would reach the age limit of thirty years, I would leave theatre forever. This time I sent in my application on time and was called,' he said.

Bashir left a week before the due date to give himself enough time to prepare for the interview. As soon as he reached Jammu, there was an announcement that Prime Minister Indira Gandhi had been assassinated. All modes of transport were brought to a halt. All trains to Delhi were cancelled. This was his first time out of Kashmir. He didn't know what else to do but wait.

'For six days, thousands of people, including me, lived on the railway station. I thought it was the will of God that I shouldn't get into NSD. On the seventh day at 7 o'clock there was an announcement that one train was to leave Jammu for Delhi. There must have been somewhere close to five thousand people on that train.'

The next morning, he reached New Delhi railway station. His interview was at 10.30 a.m. and the train arrived at around 9.30 a.m., leaving him just enough time to wash up at the station and walk down to NSD at Mandi House. 'Since I was unwashed, and I hadn't shaved in many days, during the viva one of the interviewers called me George Bernard Shaw. Also, I was wearing a saffron-coloured shirt. People at NSD thought I was some baba who had come there to collect alms,' he said.

Mohan Maharishi used to be the director of NSD then. Bashir was told that he was the only person from his state to apply. He narrated to his interviewers the entire story of how he had tried to get into NSD. He cleared that round. However, he had to appear for a final interview the next day.

'The following day, they asked me about the culture of Jammu and Kashmir. Someone asked me since I had already worked in theatre for so long what good would NSD do? I said if a glass of milk is full, adding a few petals from a rose to it wouldn't add any weight to it, only some fragrance.' By the end of the written examination and interview, he couldn't tell whether he was in or out. He had a lot of time on his hands till the results were announced. He used that time to roam around Delhi, visit the Jama Masjid, and the zoo. The results were still not announced when he left for home.

'When I reached Kashmir, I found that the news of my admission to NSD, through a letter, had reached my home before me. Alhamdulillah, I passed NSD with distinction in stagecraft and graduated in direction.' Some of Bashir's peers, such as Irrfan Khan and Mita Vashisht, would go on to earn international repute for their acting.

Did he ever meet Alkazi?

'Yes, I did, more than once. In fact, once he called for me. I went to meet Alkazi saahab in Rabindra Bhawan where, in our meeting, which must have gone on for about two or three hours, he offered me work. At NSD I used to be called "Second Alkazi" for my perfectionism. I told him I wanted to work for theatre in Kashmir and so I couldn't accept his offer. I wonder sometimes how different my life would have been had I accepted his offer.'

I asked Bashir whether he was the first from Kashmir to study at NSD. 'I was the eleventh actually. Before me many more luminaries like Shyamlal Dar Bahar, R.K. Braru, M.K. Raina, Bansi Kaul, K.K. Raina, Chandra Shekhar Raina, Virendra Razdan, Ravi Kemmu and Lateef Khatana had got in. But for twenty-five years after me, nobody from Kashmir went to NSD again.'

I asked him about M.K. Raina. Bashir said that though he was older, Bashir ended up being a junior to Raina at NSD. Raina entered NSD when he was eighteen. 'Had I got admission into NSD at his age, I would have been his senior actually,' he said, chuckling.

Bashir went on to found a drama and repertory company, Ensemble Kashmir Theatre Akademi or EKTA. They did several plays that he wrote himself and others that included *Oedipus Rex* and *Antigone* by Sophocles, *The Dumb Waiter* by Harold Pinter, *The Slave* by LeRoi Jones, *Motocar* by David Pownall, and a twenty-four-hour play adaptation of Agha Shahid Ali's *The Country Without a Post Office*. EKTA, he said, does plays that try to 'record the present tragedy', and 'show today's pains and agonies'.

'If theatre is not contemporary, it becomes irrelevant. If theatre does not stand up to the system, what will? It takes guts to stand up to something. And I continue to do my work. No threat can keep me out,' he said.

What did his roles in *Haider* and *Bajrangi Bhaijaan* do for him?

'Well, they helped me build this house, helped me get enough to eat. Otherwise how many people knew me for my theatre work?'

We finished another round of tea, and then he asked me, 'So where again did you say you were from?'

I told him.

'Yeah . . . the name Munshi does ring a bell. I knew one who used to pursue a BEd.' One after the other I gave him names, some who held high offices in administration, some who were of his age, but no name found any resonance.

It was time to take leave. '*Acha, ghar waalon ko mera aadaab kehna* [All right then, convey my greetings to your family].' We stood up and I had almost reached the door when Bashir called me back.

'Would you like to see my library?'

Of course. Nothing would give me greater pleasure.

We walked up to the only room in his house that had been left untouched by the renovation work. The one room which was remarkably clean and which he clearly loved more than the others. From the floor rose several columns of periodicals, diaries and magazines. Some topped with dusty catalogues of old Soviet-era plays. Neatly stacked in the shelves were thick annotated versions of Shakespeare's plays, books on Dara Shukoh, anthologies of Russian plays, many volumes of *Modern Indian Plays*, works of plays and criticism in Urdu, and many shelves of books by American and French playwrights. Just as I was about to leave the room, I saw placed on a shelf a collected edition of plays by Mohan Rakesh.

'Mohan Rakesh!' I said in disbelief.

'Yes, Mohan Rakesh,' said Bashir smilingly.

Immediately, two voices rang in my head.

Voice 1: 'I knew it. You were just surprised at seeing Mohan Rakesh in a *Kashmiri Muslim's* library, isn't it?'

Voice 2: 'Oh, no, no, no, no, it isn't like that. He runs a theatre here. He's studied at NSD. Of course he would have read Mohan Rakesh. Several times over. It was just that I did not expect to see the works of the Hindi playwright in Kashmir, you know. It was unexpected like . . . like . . . coming across Audrey Hepburn's name in *Aadhe Adhoore*.'

As I stepped out of his house, I glanced back at him. A smallish figure in an off-white kurta pyjama, a receding hairline that left a small patch of hair behind his ears, weary-looking eyes, and a thick white beard that gave him an imperial air. He looked ready for the stage. Fit to play the role of a crazy old man absorbed only in his art. Someone like Prospero, say, who prized his books more than his dukedom; who was about to remind us that between the two ends of the darkness that envelops us all, what mattered was our lives here on earth which were made of the stuff of dreams.

4

A Football Match in Srinagar

This happened two days before 5 August 2019, when no one had a clue why thousands of soldiers were being driven into Kashmir every day. One only had a sense of foreboding. A hunch that something new and forceful was going to hit everyone. That very soon people would be on their own. Essentials would be in short supply. At the end of whatever it was that the soldiers had come for, you could tell some families would come out in mourning. One had to be there to know how it felt. It was like being in a bus that had swerved off the road into the gorge.

I tried to hurry up with my remaining interviews. But this afternoon, nobody would meet me. I had high hopes of meeting the son of the owner of the hotel on Dal Lake where V.S. Naipaul had stayed, and which he had fondly mentioned in his India trilogy more than once. The hotel was a ten-minute ride in a shikara on the Dal. But as it turned out, the owner's son was busy taking care of some household chores. With no interviews or meetings in place, there was only one place to go.

Ever since I arrived in Srinagar, and even before that actually, I had been fascinated with how quickly Kashmir had embraced football. Within a year of its formation in 2016, the local team, Real Kashmir FC, had outperformed most other clubs in the country. It was an incredible story. In between interviews, all by myself, I would quietly watch young footballers play at the TRC football ground.

I decided to walk in and spend my afternoon watching a match. It turned out that a few matches were lined up for that day. J&K Police was playing J&K Bank. But more striking than the ongoing match and the footballers was the stand close to the entry gate. Around fifty old men were sitting in a huddle on the higher benches. I sat amidst them as they watched the game intently, chain-smoking cigarettes. An impressive-looking man, who later introduced himself as Mohammad Hanif, shouted at a passerby. 'If I don't get water—cold, chilled water—within the next ten minutes I won't come to this stadium any more.' Hanif was old, had white hair and a stubble that suggested he hadn't shaved in a couple of days, and was wearing a black Nehru jacket on top of a white kurta pyjama. But it was his restlessness that was his most striking feature.

'These people don't know how to respect real football enthusiasts,' Hanif said, speaking about the person he had just addressed, who was apparently part of the local stadium management. Hanif loved the game but he had nothing except contempt for the footballers of the day. 'Those days we used to play four football matches back-to-back and still not tire. Look at them now. Just look at them. That one over there is panting already. And it's not even half-time,' Hanif said.

'*Tim* player *kayt sa banan* [Those players, where will we get them now],' his friend, Abdul Aziz, said to Hanif. Who were 'those' players? I knew hockey used to be a rage in Kashmir in the '70s and early '80s, but had there really been a love for football in the valley?

'Farooq saahab,' someone said, and everyone grimaced and bit their tongues in veneration. 'Farooq Dar didn't run. He used to glide on the turf. What headers did he score, what kicks! Forty thousand people used to fill up Bakshi stadium just to watch him play,' Aziz said. 'People used to come even to watch him practise. He came to the SP college grounds at 6 in the morning, come hell or high water,' Hanif added.

'Not just Farooq. There were many legendary players then: Yusuf Dar, Akbar Rashid, Gulam Hassan. You won't believe what Yusuf Dar once did,' another old man sitting nearby said.

'Once, a visiting team—Jabalpur, was it?' Hanif confirmed with his friend. 'Yes. So those people with their professional boots and shin guards had come here on a tour. Our best team—Food and Supplies—was playing them. Poor guys from Food and Supplies did not even have enough money to buy themselves shoes. It was with great difficulty that they bought fleets. It was a very important match. Our pride was involved. Our first goal was very good. Habib Panzu, who was another legendary player, passed on the ball to Lach Waz, who was standing near the goal. He collected it beautifully and scored. We were 1–0 up. Then one Gul Kishan from Jabalpur scored an equalizer. Then came a gem from Yusuf Dar. He shot the ball sometime before the final whistle, with such force that it almost tore the net and came out from the other side. We won. We beat those rich upper class types 2–1,' Hanif spoke with such passion, as if he were still watching it.

'Why don't you tell him about Gul Waaza? There was this centre forward called Ghulam Rasuul Waaza in the Food and Supplies team. Once, when they were playing Transport, he shot three goals from the centre. They used to have one huge goalkeeper called Gulzar. It was from between his legs that Gul Waaza got the ball into the net. And then we had these three brothers in the Police team—Ghulam Mohammad Baba, Majeed Baba, Ghulam Nabi Baba—they used to play in the centre and demolish the defenders of the best of the teams,' Aziz interrupted.

Not even five minutes had passed before the man whom Hanif had threatened with a boycott call appeared, carrying as many mineral water bottles as his folded arms could contain. 'This is what I'm talking about. You need to respect people who respect the game,' Hanif said proudly.

'*Manzas gas yaar myanya* [Move to the middle, brother],' he shouted at a footballer who was standing his ground close to us. In his youth, Hanif used to work as a bus driver. But when it came to watching football matches, he would often drive empty buses just to get to the stadium in time. 'I've travelled all the way to Delhi and bought a ticket in black for Rs 20—it used to be a huge amount in those days—just to be able to watch a match between India and this other team whose name I can't presently recall,' Hanif said, recalling his youth. Hanif was, like most of his friends, in his early seventies. One of his comrades, who had many missing teeth, whistled to a player who had lost the ball to a footballer from the other team, 'Hey *kyoho chuk karaan* [Hey, what're you doing]?'

The mood in the football stadium was as upbeat as one could imagine. The love of football here is clearly not a passing fad. 'Football used to be everyone's first love here. But when insurgency broke out in the eighties, all forms of culture, music and art, and sport, were stopped. Some very young and talented footballers took to arms and never returned,' Hanif said.

'It was a very bad time. We had a lot of talented Kashmiri Pandit footballers as well. In fact, it was a Kashmiri Pandit who managed and organized sports in the '70s and really nurtured football when no one knew about it. But the Pandits left. One of them we called Batt Djinn [Rice Monster], I don't know his real name. But I do recall Mohan Lal, Ambarnath, Bhushanlal, Om Prakash, some of them were very good friends,' he continued.

It was now close to the final whistle and neither team had been able to score a goal. By unanimous vote, the match was declared hopeless. Hanif took out a bundle of photos from his pocket and handed them over to me. 'This person right in the front,' he said, pointing to a footballer running towards the camera with the ball, 'he's Farooq Dar.' The photo was dated

20 June 1975. The background was full of pale little dots—thousands of spectators. Farooq Dar could be seen running alone in the foreground with a little white blur that was the football. Everyone tried to get their hands on the photograph. Someone asked Hanif for more. He took out one more old, worn-out photograph. It was captioned 'J&K XI Team at Pandit Jawaharlal Nehru's House During Durand Cup'. Nehru, India's first prime minister, could be seen with the state's football team. The players were wearing dark blazers on top of white shirts. Many sported Raj Kumar–style narrow moustaches. He must have been a big style influence in those years. Some of them were beaming with pride, others looked at the camera sternly.

Hanif and his friends said they came to the football stadium every day. Sometimes even when there were no matches. 'The thing is, it is a bit stifling inside homes. What do you do back home? Sit and get frustrated. Someone will come and discuss politics. Someone else will involve you in a domestic dispute. People see you sitting by your side in old age and they start judging you. What to do? So we come here and sit through the day on one pretext or another and enjoy football. Here people know us. Even the players know us and respect us,' Hanif said.

But didn't their prolonged absence worry their families?

'They're used to it. Look at Aziz, he told his family he's gone to buy vegetables. Ha ha ha. What do we do? Football is our first love. We feel lively here. You understand? There are times when all this is shut because of some violence. Those times are the worst. There is nowhere to go. Nothing to do.'

The stands on the other side of the field were filled with men and young boys. It looked like a lot of fathers had brought their children along. On the top row of one stand, all by themselves, I saw around five girls quietly sitting and watching the match. One of them, with cropped hair, wearing sports shoes and sweat bands, seemed to be an athlete herself. Her name was Nadiya Nighat. She was twenty-two years old.

'Yes, I do play football. Actually, I'm the first female coach of the state,' Nighat said.

'I started playing in 2007. It was cricket that I used to play earlier. Someone who understands the game said I had good footwork and suggested that I switch to football. I have been playing since. There were no girls playing when I started. Now there are twelve girls' teams. I'm quite proud of what we have been able to do here,' she said.

'In times of curfew, I used to play inside my home. Sometimes, boys used to tease me. They'd say, "Look, here is this girl playing a boy's game." I cut my hair short to look more like a boy in order to be treated as an equal. I think I play better than a lot of them now.'

The Police versus Bank match finished in a goalless draw. The crowds appeared bored but they waited as two new teams took to the ground. I walked out of the stadium where everyone—including the footballers, the spectators, that man from the organizing committee—seemed to believe that they were part of something special. But all of them perhaps also knew that it wasn't likely to last very long. A day earlier, the government had issued an urgent advisory to all visitors to Kashmir to leave immediately. It made this little excursion more memorable. For a long time after the curfew was imposed, when those old men and young girls must have been confined to their homes, this football ground may have been all that they had in the way of hope.

5

A Train to the Past

It was at the Srinagar railway station that I met Sanjeet Singh Sodhi. Not at the platform, mind you, where I spent twenty minutes waiting for the train, listening to announcers issue repeated warnings about pickpockets.

'*Sawariyon se guzaarish kee jaati hai ki wo apni jebon ka khaas khayaal rakhein* [Passengers are requested to be extra careful about their pockets]', '*Sawaariyon se fir guzaarish kee jaati hai ki wo apni jebon ka khaas khayal rakhein* [Passengers are again requested to be extra careful about their pockets]', '*Sawaariyon se ek baar fir guzaarish kee jaati hai* . . . [Passengers are once again requested . . .].'

I looked around, but couldn't find any suspicious characters. It was a bright and beautiful day. Blue skies, cool air, green hills, clean surroundings, and a lot of self-absorbed passengers. They all had somewhere to go. I had a lot of time to spare and no particular destination in mind. All I wanted was to take a few rides around. Railway stations on this line, which connects Jammu's Banihal to north Kashmir's Baramulla through Srinagar, are as small and dull as those in tier-two or tier-three cities in the mainland. No Wheeler's bookshops, no tea stalls, no railway staff even. Just two bare platforms at the extremities of which armed soldiers stare at each other all day long.

I met Sodhi on the train, which arrived ten minutes after it was supposed to. As soon as the train came roaring in, the crowd lost its composure. People tried to get in at the same time that people inside were trying to get out. A kind of equilibrium was established. After a few seconds, some policemen intervened and the deadlock ended, and I found a place at the back of the chair car. In the seats ahead, I could see the back of the other passengers' heads, some turbaned, some skull-capped, some covered with abayas, some with dupattas, some full of hair, some with little left, some tilting towards other tilting heads, some looking up, others resting on arms balanced on handrails. The heads would turn slightly with the arrival of a dry fruit vendor or a juice vendor. The salesmen of rare ointments, fancy herbs and religious threads that I'd come across the last time I had boarded a train on this line were nowhere to be seen.

I looked around my coach. I wanted to talk to someone about what this public transport meant to them. More than a decade after its launch, the trains have been running smoothly, ferrying passengers from Jammu to towns in south, central and north Kashmir. And doing so in the shortest possible time and in the cheapest way possible, bypassing traffic, curfews and pickets on the road. But nobody around me seemed to be in a mood to talk. Then I spotted a man in a blue turban. He had a full black beard, checked shirt, black trousers and a slight paunch. He seemed cheerful, full of energy, full of love for life. He was Sanjeet Singh Sodhi.

'At least we reach home on time when we are on this train. On the road you can't tell when you'll get stuck in traffic or a curfew. It is really cheap as well. I pay a daily fare of Rs 20 that would cost me Rs 180 by road. Through the train I reach in 1.5 hours, by road it takes me nothing less than five hours to reach Baramulla,' he said.

What memories did he have of travelling in this train? What stood out when he looked back over the last ten years?

'Initially there were many protests, some people broke the window panes with stones, only to freeze in harsh winters when they were travelling in it themselves. But people have accepted it now and this train has become part of our lives. Though hygiene is a problem here. People here take little time in dirtying the coaches. Just look around,' he said, pointing to heaps of empty peanut shells. 'Thank god they don't serve tea here.'

I asked him about his life in Kashmir, his home, his childhood.

'I was born in Uplina, in Baramulla's Singhpora area. My father was in the state horticulture department, my mother was a teacher. After finishing my schooling here, I went to a college in Uttar Pradesh where I did my BSc.'

What else did he remember about growing up in Kashmir?

'Crackdowns. Lots of crackdowns. And curfews.'

'Crackdown'. The word isn't quite as straightforward as most of its bisyllabic relatives one comes across in news reports on Kashmir: gunfire, shot dead, brute force, bloodshed. It doesn't even get close to describing what it does to the people who are subjected to a 'Crackdown'. Kashmiri writers and artists have defined it repeatedly through lived experience—Basharat Peer in *Curfewed Night*, Mirza Waheed in *The Collaborator* and Malik Sajad in *Munnu: A Boy from Kashmir*. As in this case did Sanjeet Singh:

'The army would ask all the men to vacate their houses and assemble at the local eidgah from 6 in the morning till 8 in the evening. The women were left behind. For these fourteen hours, they would search houses for weapons and look for anyone who might be involved with the terror groups. Sometimes it continued for days on end. In summers and in winters. There were 100 families in our locality of which only three, including mine, were Sikhs. Sometimes the senior army officials on duty would offer to make concessions for us. Let us be in our homes during crackdowns. But it was unacceptable to my father. He would say that we all should go with the other men to show solidarity.'

Sanjeet Singh's father may have joined the rest of his townsmen out of empathy, even when he needn't have exposed himself to such discomfort. But the reasons for walking away from their houses, leaving behind women and children, as soldiers marched towards them, may not have been the same for all Sikhs. In Srinagar's Mehjoor Nagar, where six Sikhs were gunned down in February 2001, a Sikh remembered crackdowns a little differently.

'Yes, we did go out with the rest of our neighbourhood, but it wasn't only out of a sense of solidarity. Though there was a close bond. And having seen and occasionally felt the wrath of the forces, we could imagine how it must be for those boys . . . But the fact is that we were just a handful of Sikh families. If we did not assemble with the rest of the town during those crackdowns, we would have been seen as collaborators. That we couldn't afford.'

The anxieties of a living through a crackdown were as real for Sikhs as they were for the local Muslims. 'There was this one day, in the early '90s, when Muslim women came out to protest against the continuing crackdowns . . . these things could really take a toll on your mental health, make you really desperate . . . the soldiers came to subdue them. One of the women tried to snatch a rifle, and she was shot, more women clashed. Bullets were flying all over the place. We thought we would die that day, but nothing happened to us eventually. In the evening, we came to know that seven people had died that day,' Sanjeet Singh said.

He was in the ninth standard when he first heard gunfire, he recalls. 'A group of soldiers were attacked in Azadgunj near the old cement bridge, I still remember. There was a lot of firing, grenade explosions and stone throwing. At that time I didn't know what to make of it. Then it happened when I was in my BSc final year—the Chhattisinghpora massacre.'

It was one of the deadliest spells of violence in Kashmir. In South Kashmir's Anantnag district on an evening in March 2000, 35 Sikhs were lined up in two rows and shot dead. It really shook the community from within. Many Sikhs, like Pandits, decided to pack their bags and leave.

'In those moments, we were thinking of leaving. We had our bags packed. If we were going to be pulled into this conflict and butchered then we couldn't survive here any more. We said this to our elders. But somehow things changed. A day or so after the incident, our seniors told us that we shouldn't leave. The government had promised us safety. So we went back to living the way we were. But it wasn't like before . . . Sometimes I wonder whether we really should have left. We would have made something for ourselves and our children,' the Sikh man at the Mehjoor Nagar gurudwara said.

With him was another Sikh man who said that while his community was rattled, it did not lose faith. There were even some moments of courage. 'After this incident, things continued to go from bad to worse. We had these militants come to our neighbourhood almost every other night and demand money. There was this one night when a couple of them came. We had no money to give them. We were fed up with them. When we approached them pleading to be left alone, they pointed their rifles at us and threatened to shoot. There was this elderly Sikh woman who lived not very far from here. God bless her soul. She walked up to one of them and gave him such a tight slap that the rifle fell from his hands. She picked it up and threatened to shoot both of them. Both of them started begging for their lives. No one knew where she got this strength from. But that night something changed within us. We never lived in fear from that night onwards. We have held our heads high ever since.'

I remembered leaving the gurudwara at Mehjoor Nagar while a young Sikh couple was making their way in, a few days before 5 August. The two had come to seek blessings before getting married at a time of severe tensions and uncertainty in the valley. I asked Sanjeet what he made about the prospects of the younger generation.

The summit of the Habba Khatoon peak lit up by the dying rays of the sun.

People praying at St Joseph's Church, Baramulla, on Christmas day.

The Bund in Srinagar curves along the Jhelum river, with Zero Bridge seen in the distance.

Basheer Ahmad Bhagat, from the well-known indigenous street theatre group Kashmir Bhagat Theatre, at his home, showing the awards he and his family have won.

Elderly football enthusiasts enjoying a game at TRC stadium, Srinagar.

The octagonal tank around the Verinag spring which is believed to
have been built by Mughal emperor Jahangir.

Madhosh Balhami at his house in Pulwama district, narrating one of his poems.

O.N. Bhat's is the lone Pandit family left in Hal, Shopian.

After two days of heavy rainfall, during which time the Bakarwal nomadic shepherds were mostly cooped up in their tents, the sun finally came out and we were greeted with this beautiful rainbow.

Nazeer with his brother Riyaz (left) at the camp in Hirpora, Shopian, one morning.

Rabeena trying to light a fire near her tent after a gruelling trek down the Pir Panjal mountains.

Shakil (left) and Liyaqat enjoying their time together.

A few hours after we crossed the Pir Panjal mountains, Majeed walks on with the herd.

The Bakarwals and their herd a little way up Hirpora.

A photo of the entire Bakarwal group, on the author's last day with them.

A young Bakarwal, waiting with his dog for the rest of the caravan to catch up.

'When they go outside they see movie halls, they see people happily moving around, they see momos, they get a taste for these things. What do they have here? *Jahnam* [Hell],' he says. I smile at his use of the word. A Kashmiri is likely to be condemned, or condemn themselves, to eternal damnation in 'Jahnam', no matter what their faith.

Has he ever thought of going somewhere himself?

'Where will we go? We've spent all our lives here only. And this is where we'll take our last breaths. Yes, once in a while we take a trip to Jammu but that's about it . . . One tends to go overboard on eating and feasting there . . . it is much better in the valley,' he said, laughing.

We had covered a good distance. It was 5.20 p.m., and we were about to reach the railway station at Sopore. Outside, the scenery had changed from large, undulating fields to rougher, uneven earth.

'*Wasun chuv*?' Sanjeet Singh Sodhi asked two young girls wearing hijabs whether they meant to get down. The train was about to enter the railway station at Sopore. The two nodded, stood up and walked towards the door where they joined the long queue of other passengers waiting to get off, while we took their seats. It was not the first time I heard a Sikh speak Kashmiri. But every time, it sounds a bit strange, maybe because I grew up without hearing or seeing any Kashmiri Sikh speak the language. It seems surprising the same way that very young children talking in Kashmiri used to surprise me. When, some seven years ago, for the first time I heard a little boy chatter in Kashmiri, I felt a sense of wonder. Having grown up in a family that did not encourage its children to speak in Kashmiri, I had somehow related the speaking of it only with adults. It hadn't occurred to me that children could exchange private jokes in it, that they could sing songs in Kashmiri.

After our exodus, some Pandit families had decided to speak to their children only in Hindi and English, to give them a metropolitan upbringing. Times were tough. The displaced families counted on the children to shed their provincial ways and compete with the world on equal terms. While it became easier for us to catch up with the rest of the classroom, we lost the only vehicle through which age-old traditions and culture could be acquired, practised and passed on. Exodus has meant different things to different people. Those of us who can see the sun set on our culture, who can see, within our own lifetimes, our culture drawing nearer toward the darkness into which many civilizations, languages and traditions have disappeared forever, live with a hopelessness that is hard to express. But the Pandits have been through much worse—we have seen the reign of tyrants, natural disasters like floods, famines, and spells of cholera—and yet, here we are.

'*Ek time tha Kashmiri chaku se bhi darta tha . . . agar kisi gali mein kisiko chaku dikh bhi gaya, wahan koi ek hafte tak nahi jaata tha. Ek time aisa bhi tha* [There was a time when a Kashmiri was scared of even a knife . . . if someone was threatened with a knife in an alley, nobody would go there for a week. There were such times as well],' Sanjeet said, looking out from his window.

So what changed?

'Unemployment. Young people don't have jobs these days,' he said, waving at a man selling peanuts. 'This guy selling peanuts, he's an MA [Master of Arts], BEd [Bachelor of Education]. Just look at him.' The guy, a young man wearing a T-shirt and jeans, came towards Sanjeet. 'What all have you studied, please tell him,' he said to the young man. 'MA, BEd,' the young man responded with a concision that seemed to have been achieved by rote. Now that he had been introduced to me, the only natural thing was to introduce myself. I gave my name to him and said that I was working on a book. The boy darted out of the coach. 'He is a little shy sometimes,' Sanjeet said.

Soon, we reached Baramulla. It was the end of our long conversation. I wondered how, when he returned home, he would recount our conversation to his family. It was amazing to me that through all this turmoil Sikhs should still be living in Kashmir, still be calling it their home. That they should sometimes feel wronged but not necessarily out of place.

I ran for the ticket counter that Sanjeet had directed me towards. This was the last train back to Srinagar. In time I managed to get a return ticket. The train was quite empty this time. I took a window seat. We were back in Sopore in no time. As soon as people climbed the train, a policeman sauntering on the platform spotted a rucksack. Someone had left it behind. On purpose?

'*Oye, ye bag kiska hai* [Whose bag is this]?' the policeman shouted. Nobody responded. The policeman picked it up. I felt my heart skip a beat. He was standing maybe 10 feet away from me. The train started to move as he began looking into it, sifting through its contents. Why would he do that? I'll never know.

SOUTH KASHMIR

1

Reaching Out to Kids in Anantnag

It was a busy market day in Anantnag town. My friend and I were making our way through the rush to meet the editor of a children's magazine. At a street corner, a tall, heavily built man with a faint, long scar on his face had gathered a sizeable crowd. He was in the final stages of mixing some herbs in a thick, dark jam.

'*Yi banyav, jenaab, majun-e-chobchini. Yi banyav majun-e-muqawwi. Yi banyav chawanfrash. Yi banyav, janeb-e-ali, chawanfrash sund mol,*' he said, vigorously mixing the jam with two large spoons, while taking the names of the herbs that had lent the potion its qualities. What he left unsaid, but which was understood and had silently attracted a small crowd of middle-aged men, was that he was preparing a tonic to cure impotency.

Khalid Fayaz, the editor of the children's magazine *Zaanvun Lokchaar* (Knowing Childhood), was waiting for us in a restaurant. He had started this project in December 2017. The tone of the magazine was far from being patronizing. Children were addressed as equals. I suppose this must have meant a lot to the readers.

We met on the first floor of the restaurant. The twenty-six-year-old had the confidence of someone at least a decade older than himself. The authority with which he spoke to the waiters, the purpose with which he carried himself on the streets, the spontaneity with which he answered questions, it felt like watching someone trying to leap through the years. I wanted to understand how exactly he was trying to distract children, who were growing up witnessing gore and gun battles, with literature and ideas. I also wanted to know how the children were responding to his ideas. Such a project requires an abundance of self-belief. I asked him about the impulse that made him start the magazine.

'When we started this magazine, we had just one thing in mind. We wanted to connect students to their own surroundings. What happens is that when you're born in a conflict zone like Kashmir, you automatically get attached to a political view. We wanted to undo this. Our goal was to bring out those narratives or stories of children that were getting silenced in the clash of well-known narratives. We recently did an issue on video games. We wanted to tell students how they're beneficial, just to challenge the popular opinion against them. Most of the existing magazines here are recycling the same clichés. And I'm not saying all this out of pride,' Fayaz said.

Fayaz claims that *Lokchaar* sells between 3000 to 5000 copies in a month. Among other things, the editions carry quizzes on Kashmir—number of major rivers, tallest peak, local fruits and so on. 'We did a whole issue on apples. A French girl who is a contributor to our magazine came to our office one day and made an apple pie for us. We were stunned. We have apples everywhere but it did not occur to any of us until that moment that we could make apple pies.'

Still, what the children of Kashmir are most interested in, he has found, is conflict and religion. 'You cannot escape the elephant in the room,' he said.

'We had to put a halt to accepting contributions from children for some time because most of the poems were political poems. Hardcore political.'

Like what?

'Like on the Kathua rape case. Students, especially a few girls from Sopore, sixth to ninth standard, even twelfth standard, we found, were sending only political stuff. One of the students in seventh standard sent us a poem on the Sopore massacre.'*

The contributions surprised Fayaz. He was surprised that the girl could have drawn such sharp and vivid imagery about an incident that had occurred years before she was born. After reading several such submissions he realized how many children across the valley were suffering from unaddressed, inherited trauma, apart from those they had personally suffered.

'The reason, it occurred to me later, was that because she had lived in Sopore for so long, she couldn't escape its history. She was dealing with the same demons that her parents had dealt with and would perhaps pass them on to her own children as well . . .'

In 2017, I had interviewed Dr Arshad Hussain, a leading psychiatrist and associate professor, psychiatry at Government Medical College, Srinagar. Dr Arshad and his team had just finished a study on mental health in the valley and found that 90 per cent of Kashmiris had suffered from at least one traumatic event in their lives. He spoke about one of his patients, a ten-year-old boy who had heard gunfire and explosions around his house one night. For a month after that, he had not been able to sleep at all.

Before airing scenes of graphic violence, television channels often advise viewers to exercise their discretion. This option isn't available to people, especially children, in Kashmir.

Some children, though, are finding ways of dealing with their issues through writing. One of Fayaz's contributors, a twelfth-standard student, sent him a book she had written, a fictionalized account of living with Obsessive Compulsive Disorder (OCD).

---

* In 1993, paramilitary soldiers are alleged to have fired upon protesters in the northern Kashmiri town, burning down houses and shops. Various media reports pegged the number of casualties at around fifty.

It was an impressive attempt, said Fayaz, a book rooted, in a roundabout manner, in the conflict.

'Our society considers OCD as the devil himself. For instance when we say "*Cse goya aab-tasruff*" in Kashmiri to someone who is constantly engaging with water, we mean "You've become a water devil". When this contributor was taken to a psychiatrist, she was told that she was an "OCD patient". Now when you're classified as a "patient", you get socially stigmatized. That she wouldn't get married would be the first casualty to her parents. Also, when you say she's a "patient", you're disengaging her from her intelligence. She was compelled to write, write, write, and then she revealed herself. She thought she was ill but it turned out otherwise. I tell the highfalutin writers here, if you're quoting anyone, you should quote Carl Jung because he at least lived that life, of seeing mental illnesses in his family from up close. That kind of philosophy we need to encourage.'

Fayaz's impatience in this context with the parents, especially, shows in a note addressed to 'All the parents' in one issue of *Lokchaar*.

'Have you ever noticed that your child has started talking more than before? At midnight, have you ever checked if your child is really sleeping or pretending to do so? In the morning, have you ever seen the tear marks on their pillows because of their crying all night? Have you ever noticed their silence and that always-angry behaviour? No, you haven't. Because it doesn't suit your comfort zone, isn't it?'

He said that he didn't want his contributors to take borrowed tragedies and make poems out of them. 'We want children to write on the arts, on history, on food, on literature. We sometimes get short stories. One student sent us a pamphlet called "Seven Betrayals of Kashmir". It was a jumble of clichés. Still, we are engaging with him. I'm sure all these children will in time shift their focus to culture.'

An issue of *Lokchaar* carries the winning entry of the children's writing competition for that month. It's 'A Letter to Allah' written by a fourth-standard girl. The letter is a list of question that the girl says she has always been thinking about, such as, 'How does it feel to be the king of everyone?', 'People who don't believe in You but do good deeds, will they go to Jannah?', 'If Adam (PBUH) made a small mistake and then asked for forgiveness, then why did you send us all down here to earth?', 'Why have you not sent any women as a Prophet?'

Through the magazine, Fayaz runs a book club of sorts. He invites young people of all age groups to discuss the books they like.

'We did some book reviews in our magazines to rekindle children's interest in literature. We reviewed *The Alchemist* since a lot of children had heard about it. Then we moved to Frantz Fanon and others. There were people eighteen and above who wanted to read and discuss him. Then we started reviewing articles and poems sent to us by our contributors.'

I wondered aloud if there were any no-go zones in his magazine, because the words 'children', 'book', 'writing' and 'Kashmir' had immediately brought to mind Salman Rushdie. He had written two books for children, dedicated to his two sons. He was born into a Kashmiri family and had written quite a bit about the valley. In fact he, and to an extent Agha Shahid Ali, had introduced Kashmir and its culture to the world. And yet, his superb novel *The Satanic Verses* had made him one of the most hated people in Kashmir. I asked Fayaz if he would ever publish Rushdie.

'Why not? If you read our religion section, you will get to know. We did a piece on an imagined conversation between a maulvi and a Sufi who are talking about dogs in Islam. We challenged the prevalent bias in Muslims about dogs being impure. Such prejudice and ignorance are exactly what we write against. We have tried to create space for rational dialogue. If you're engaging in a rational dialogue then why not? We have an editorial policy not to publish anything that's narrowly political. Our only demand from our contributors is that their pieces should focus on Kashmir. We have contributors from Germany and France, but we have told them that the focus should be Kashmir. We don't have any other bias.' There, Rushdie has his work cut out.

Fayaz's emotions spring forth when he speaks of the contributions he gets from mainland India on Kashmir. 'I have one problem with "Indians", per se, those who are trying to engage themselves with Kashmir. Those writers want to talk either on the lines that the government is taking, so it is futile, because people here don't accept it. Then you have rational writers like Arundhati Roy. Again, they sound sort of patronizing to us. Why don't these people intervene to prevent soldiers from coming here? When your army leaves for Kashmir, just stop them . . . I mean which war are you fighting? Like when Americans stopped their army from going to Vietnam. Why can't they do that . . . if they're so liberal?'

Yet, for all his rants about its futility, writing was what he was engaged in. It was the medium through which he was trying to wean children away from the reality of violence into the world of creativity. There was a challenge, though. There were very few bookstores in the valley. If he wanted children to discuss and analyse books and culture at large, how was he going to do it in the absence of bookstores, and with long and frequent Internet shutdowns?

'It's true that in Kashmir you'll find at every street corner barbeque vendors, dress shops, bakers, but no bookshops. This shows where, as a society, we're going. Maybe that barbeque vendor down your street is the only space currently left for you to discuss new ideas. Maybe your food is the last remaining thing that is still unoccupied. The absence of bookshops in Kashmir is more worrying when you see a new generation coming into its own. A new crop of youngsters with only a past and the present, and a future which offers nothing.'

From the window one could see the bustle of shoppers and traders in the marketplace below. This was the last week of July 2019. Fayaz managed to borrow another hour from a waiter who was growing impatient with a table that he was not serving. I asked him, to lighten the mood, if his magazine had published anything funny lately.

'We do publish humour. We recently included in one of our recent issues an actual incident that had happened quite close to this place: There was an Ikhwan* in our area who would pick up anyone and demand money in exchange for their release. Once, he picked a carpenter and asked him to count the number of windows in a large house. For each window, the Ikhwan demanded, the carpenter would have to pay Rs 10. It was not a small amount in those days. The carpenter counted twelve windows and paid the Ikhwan Rs 120. After being released, when people asked the carpenter why he had let go of his savings so easily, he said, laughing, 'I fooled him. There were eighteen windows in the house.'

'I don't know where you'd place this humour, in conflict or in everyday life? Or does this seem like a cliché to you?'

Not since George Orwell—who was acutely alert to and persuasive about the connection between the sloppy writer and the lurking fascist—was anyone so hung up as Fayaz on the idea of clichés. Even as we placed a few orders in the restaurant to be able to buy some more time, Fayaz's cliché-detector kept tripping on his own self. 'I'll have tea with butter toast, thank you . . . See, this is a cliche also.' But one understood why he instinctively recoiled at what he called 'borrowed tragedies'.

Kashmir is an impossible project. It is a tragedy that isn't running out of performers, acts, plots, sub-plots, even thirty years after the violence began. The troupe is also the audience. You have to play not just your own part but memorize everyone else's lines too. In which year did such and such event unfold? Who said what, to whom, on which date? Remember that pain, that rush of blood?

---

* Pro-government militia, who broke the back of the militancy in the 1990s and were accused, like the militants themselves, of repeatedly abusing human rights.

Or should you rather forget it? It is an unending spiral. Your best chance at sanity is maybe to get as far from it as you can, as early as you can.

I feel that Fayaz, and many others like him, realize this. And by trying to engage the newer generation in creative pursuits, in self-expression, in newer thoughts, they're helping them outrun the plot.

2

To the Spring of Verinag

My next stop was the house of Basheer Ahmad Bhagat. He is the leading light of one of the valley's most known Bhand Pather or indigenous street theatre groups, the Kashmir Bhagat Theatre. The Bhands have engaged with Kashmiri society for so long that they have become part of its cultural history. It is incredible that they are still around, shouldering a tradition that has thrived on entertaining the public by mocking the high and the mighty.

However, before I met Basheer, I wanted to take a short trip to Kashmir's southern end, to the spring of Verinag, the birthplace of the Jhelum.

I had read much about its beauty. The original spring with marsh around it is said to have caught the eye of the Mughal emperor Jahangir. He fenced it with an octagonal tank and laid beautiful gardens around it at the beginning of the seventeenth century. Shah Jahan is said to have finished work on it and grown so fond of it that he wished in his dying breath for Verinag to be his final resting place. In his book *Jhelum: The River Through My Backyard*, Khalid Bashir Ahmad notes that Shah Jahan's contemporary, Francisco Pelsaert, a Dutch Protestant in the service of the Dutch East India Company, had written that Verinag was 'the most delightful pleasure resort where the King had the best hunting grounds in the whole of India'.[1]

Shonaleeka Kaul in *The Making of Early Kashmir*[2] quotes twelfth-century Kashmiri poet Kalhana, who described Verinag's place in Kashmir in these words: 'The territory which is under the protection of Nila, supreme lord of all the nagas (tutelary spring deities), whose parasol is the swelling Nila kunda (spring; the modern-day Verinag) with the flowering waters of the Vitasta [Jhelum] for its staff.'

Verinag was a short distance from Anantnag, about 30 kilometres, which started with an uphill drive. It was quite rewarding. Away from the haze of the small town, we were climbing up towards clearer, bluer skies. Soon, we reached Shahbad, which is known as the hometown of nineteenth-century poet Rasul Mir. His flamboyant poems celebrating love remain in currency even now. The village Dooru welcomes visitors with a huge, flat-arched entrance gate bearing, in bold letters, one of his most famous quatrains:

> *Rasul Mir chhui shahabad Durey,*
> *Am chhu trovmut aeshka dukan.*
> *Yeevo ashkow cheyiv turi turay.*
> *Mein chu moorey lalvun naar*
> [This is Rasool Mir of Shahabad Dooru
> He has opened a shop of tears.
> Come, lovers, drink cupfuls away.
> I have to nurture the fire of love everyday]

In another half an hour, we reached Verinag. It was smaller than what I had pictured in my mind. And at first glance, it looked like Srinagar's Nishat Bagh. That is, until I absorbed my surroundings. Having gained some elevation, we were now covered by a sky which was as blue as a placid ocean. Against this deep blue, at the far end of Verinag, rose a lush green hill. There were so many trees on the hill that it looked like they had been swept up into a heap. This was the backdrop to the garden through which ran a small stream, all along which stood mighty old Chinar trees. God knows how long they had been around, and what all they had seen. Who knows, Rasul Mir may have composed his 'Rinda Posha Mal' in these very gardens, with no clue that one day, it would become a popular dance number.

There were many schoolchildren around, busy throwing each other into the stream. On bedsheets spread wide under Chinar trees lay several elderly people. The shade of a Chinar, it is often said in our house, is something worth dying for.

It was hard to believe that the stream that flowed beside the Chinar trees later takes on the volume and ferocity of a river many times its size. But I was told that this was just one of the many streams that eventually merged into what we know as the Jhelum. The spring itself was huge and full of pale turquoise water so clear you could easily see the fish swimming several feet below. The depth of this spring is believed to have remained more or less the same since it was built.

I walked by the water. There were small hollow arcs built into the wall surrounding the spring. Some of them were empty but one housed a Shivling. Another had a weather-beaten idol. They reminded me of primitive statuettes I had seen in a temple in Trehgam in north Kashmir several years ago.

As I started towards the exit, on the other side of the stream, I saw a man trying to dip his toe into the flowing water. Next to him were two women, most likely family members. They looked like tourists. I wasn't sure, but they were probably Kashmiri Pandits. They looked the part—the man had a lampshade moustache and the women were wearing bindis. If they were indeed Pandits, then it was remarkable that they had ventured so far out of the city. A 'Namaskaar' and another 'Namaskaar' in return usually puts an end to such speculations. But shouting a 'Namaskaar' from across the stream would have sounded a bit odd. Also, I realized I had been staring at them absent-mindedly all this while. All three were now stealing glances at me with increasing wariness. The first impression had been soured; it was best to leave them alone. I looked away and kept walking. The time had come to leave for the house of Basheer Ahmad Bhagat.

3

Playing Shakespeare in Mohripora

'*Chai banaavsa asal pahaan* [Make some nice tea],' Basheer Ahmad Bhagat said to no one in particular as we walked into his house. '*Asi che pyets aamit* [We have guests].'

Basheer was more than eager to talk about his profession, one of the oldest in the valley. Street theatre artists or *bhands* entertain people through sketches based on folk tales or *pather*.

'We used to tell the stories when there was no media. We used to tell people about their background. Tell them about their history,' Basheer said, '*Pashe Manzar* [The yesteryears] . . . *Nichod* [The crux of their history] . . . You get it?'

But this form of street play wasn't just about entertainment. It was a form of protest. The street artists before Bhagat had created 'Darz Pather', stories about the excesses committed by the Dard community when hundreds of years back they used to lord over Kashmir. They created 'Angrez Pather', stories lampooning the Raj. 'We had "Raj Pather" to mock the kings of the day. It may sound strange but the same people we criticized were also our patrons. *Huquumat se paisa leke unhi ki nuqta-cheeni karte the* [We took money from the rulers, the same people whom we used to criticise].'

Bhands were armed with a licence to lampoon everyone. Their main audience was in the villages, which was why their object of ridicule was the ruling class. Bhands didn't perform from prepared scripts. The actors would agree on a general theme and improvise on the spot. This had its disadvantages but was also a defining feature of the genre. Much before the entry of television, these roving Bhand Pather troupes were the only source not just of entertainment but of information as well for the common people. When they were not touring, they would perform at weddings, festivals and political rallies. About 125 years ago, this is what Walter Roper Lawrence wrote about the bhands in *Valley of Kashmir*:[1]

> It is probably due to the Kashmiri's inaptitude for active amusement that the strolling players, the *Band* or *Bhaggat*, have such a hold on the people. These players, who are well known in India, are enthusiastically received and their wit and power of mimicry entitle them to a warm reception.

Lawrence uses the name 'Bhaggat' as a synonym for bhands, which is probably a fair indication of how dominant the Bhagats were in the field. He goes on:

> I have seen the best companies in Kashmir, though perhaps the best—the Bhaggats of Syebug—died off in the famine of 1877 . . . The Bhaggats portray village life in a most vivid manner. Their dresses and make-up are excellent and they represent most faithfully the internal working of a village community. It is said that Maharaja Gulab Singh acquired a very intimate knowledge of village administration from the Bhaggats' performances and I have picked up some hints from them as to the methods of the patwari, the village accountant.'

The Bhands, Lawrence adds, 'relieve the sadness of village life in Kashmir.'

Basheer Ahmad Bhagat's family officially started performing Bhand Pathers in 1959. The founding member of the group was Ghulam Rasool Bhagat, who went on to win a Sangeet Natak Akademi award. 'He was a man full of ideas. He helped popularize Bhand Pather on stage as well as on radio. The great theatre director and playwright M.L. Kemmu helped formalize the whole thing. We even started getting some government patronage. But just when we had started to stand on our feet, militancy broke out in the valley.'

A tradition that had flowed through centuries dried up within days. Bhands disappeared from public squares. The religious hardliners, who were now calling the shots, didn't like the idea of people singing and dancing, probably because it was their turn to be mocked. So the Bhands quietly vanished.

'It was our desire to keep performing during those days also. In fact, we felt that performing street plays was more urgently needed then. But we didn't perform out of fear. One by one, we had to sell all the theatre equipment. Some of us became cooks, some were hired as daily-wage labourers. Shehnai used to be a central item in our plays. *Shehnai hamara ek aham item hota tha. Un dino lagta tha Shehnai mar gai. Hum log andar hi andar mar rahe the.* [In those days of violence it felt like the Shehnai had been silenced. And with it all of us],' Basheer says. Though he quickly adds, 'Not that anyone personally threatened us. It was we who felt that it wasn't safe to go around like before.'

But a tradition that had perhaps seen far greater adversities couldn't be wished away in a few days, or months or years, by some people with guns. It flowed again.

'See, we are illiterate people. We used to do our shows without scripts. It was all impromptu stuff. Then M.K. Raina (an acclaimed actor and director), who is my guru, came and worked with us for a long time. He made us more professional in our approach, asked us to work on newer themes. He taught us playwrighting. He mentored us on a Badshah Pather that was based on King Lear.'

According to some reports, on 29 April 2011, a large crowd gathered to watch Kashmir Bhagat Theater's adaptation of *King Lear* in south Kashmir's Akingam. It was a huge hit. 'After doing twelve shows in Kashmir, we took the Badshah Pather to theatre festivals across the country. We did nearly 300 shows of it, 150 of them just in Assam. Can you believe it! They couldn't even understand our dialogues but the crowds loved it.' It was a great time for Basheer and his troupe.

'You travel across the country and you are surprised by how different people are. We went to do these shows in some interior villages of Rajasthan. The nearest city, Jodhpur, was several hours away. Those people, our audience, were quite poor. They didn't even have electricity. It was quite hot in those days. And without fans or coolers, it was quite unbearable. But the way they treated us! I can't tell you how much they loved us. They kept asking us whether we had eaten properly. Whether we needed anything. I can't forget that night. It was like we were back in Kashmir. The next day, none of us wanted to leave.'

How does Badhsah Pather start?

'*Dekho sitart Badshah ke khandar se hota hai* [It starts in the ruins of the King's castle].' And then the play, Basheer says, goes on to talk about how the king's sons, who he loved more than anyone else, betray him one by one.

Wait. King Lear didn't have any sons. He had daughters.

'Yes, I know, but in our culture we don't show women in our plays. And if it really is required, it is the men who play the female roles.'

Bhagat, who played the role of the fool—the character for whom Shakespeare often reserved the best lines—agreed to do a small act for us. Just one line where he mocks the king, the Badshah Salaamat. He turned at an angle away from us, towards an imaginary audience, crossed his legs, held his arms high, his palms open, and started to address the king.

He had told us earlier that when they perform, bhands lose their sense of themselves. A spirit, a *ruh*, is released from within.

With equal solemnity, and marked disdain, he had also spoken about television. 'Today, most of what these people watch is Ekta Kapoor soaps. But let me tell you. You get people to switch on an Ekta Kapoor serial and give us a space nearby. I promise you that everyone will come to us. Nobody will watch television any more.'

Basheer launched into his act:

'Badshah Salamaat! Teym saatan katy aes chayn akal yel tse panyin saltanat yemin athye dyitseth, te panyin tsakeyj dagnevuth . . . Ha ha ha ha . . . ho ho . . . ho ho . . . he he he he . . . Aaaa . . . tyem von tse—"Daziv daziv daziv. Agar shor korvu te ati kadhov jaan" . . . ha ha ha ha . . . ho ho ho ho . . . he he he he.'

[O King! What were you thinking of when you gave your sultanate to them and got your behind whipped . . . Ha ha ha ha . . . ho ho . . . he he he he . . . Yesss . . . he did say to you—"Burn burn burn. If you raise your voice I'll silence you forever" . . . ha ha ha ha . . . ho ho ho ho . . . he he he he.']

My friend and I collapsed on the floor laughing at the way he leaned forward and patted his behind (*tsakeyj*) to show the part of his body where the king had invited wrath. There were just the two of us. He didn't really need to make the effort. But he delivered those lines like an actor who had been thirsting for an audience for a long time.

Basheer's troupe still gets the occasional invitation to festivals and is able to make ends meet because of a state grant. They are luckier than the bhands Basheer had spoken about earlier, who were forced to abandon their love for street theatre and take to hard labour to support their families. Mohripora and a few villages surrounding it were once great centres of Bhand Pather.

Mohripora could easily have been the setting of Salman Rushdie's *Shalimar the Clown*, the fictional town of Pachigam 'due south of Srinagar and west of Shirmal near the Anantnag road'. The Bhand Pather troupe led by Abdullah Sher Noman, Shalimar's father, was famous for its play *Budshah*, based on the life of Zain-ul-abidin, the eighth sultan of Kashmir. 'Bud Shah', as he is more popularly known in the valley, is remembered as a tolerant, kind and culturally inclined king who brought peace and prosperity to Kashmir during his reign. That the bhands couldn't count on their performances alone for their sustenance, Abdullah knew back in the 1960s.

> Bhand Pather or clown stories were still the undisputed player kings of the valley, but Abdullah the genius—young Abdullah, in his prime—was the one who made them learn how to be cooks as well. In the valley at times of celebration people liked a bit of a drama to watch but there was also a demand for those who could prepare the legendary wazwaan . . . as Abdullah pointed out it was easier to study recipes than to hold an audience in the palm of your hand.

Just like the Nomans, the Bhagats realize that they're fighting a losing battle against technology, against the changing times. If the bhands had their way, they would have shred all the self-righteous figures in Kashmir today to pieces. But shrinking audiences and touchy administrators don't offer that luxury. Despite this, somewhere in his own private world, a bhand is still performing. Basheer Ahmad Bhagat is still challenging his audience, and his king, from his bedroom, his arms raised high, his palms held wide open.

4

The Yeats of Pulwama

I had mixed feelings about meeting Madhosh Balhami. His story had been written about in many newspapers and magazines. The metaphor of his tragedy had been mined hollow. But still, what a metaphor! A poet whose life's work, whose library, whose house had been reduced to ashes in a gunfight between militants and security forces. He had watched his house burn the whole night and composed a small verse on it:

> *Bada sharir tha umr bhar mujhe sata liya*
> *Khuda ne mere ghar se mera inteqaam liya*
> *Wo aatish-e-namrood mera kuch bigaad na sake*
> *Meri kalam na cheen sake mera qalaam liya*
> [He was vicious, all he did was torment
> Through my house, God took his revenge
> What the fires of Namrood couldn't achieve
> They did by snatching away my pen]

I called him up one morning. Was he at his home, I asked. 'Where else would you like me to be?' This was our first exchange of words.

The auto driver taking me to Balhama, a village in South Kashmir's Pulwama district, asked me for the specific location. 'We have to go to the house of Madhosh Balhami,' I said sheepishly, since my host's name literally meant an intoxicated person from Balhama. I wished I had known beforehand his real name, Ghulam Mohammad Bhat. 'Is he a *pir* baba?'

'No, he's a poet,' I said, using the Urdu word '*shayar*'.

'Shayar,' the auto driver repeated to himself.

We found Balhami's newly built house on top of a small hill. It hadn't been painted yet. I was led into a room by one of the women of the house. Balhami walked in a few minutes later. His large head, with a receding hairline and salt-and-pepper beard, rested upon a frail body. He was, in fact, a farmer. That's how the fifty-three-year-old shayar earned his living.

'My father died when I was young. My brothers left me. I was left alone to tend to my mother. This gave me my earliest sense of suffering. Then one day I listened to a recitation of Habba Khatoon's verses on radio. Her poetry was full of day-to-day household problems. That gave me the idea to write poetry,' Balhami said. He doesn't think poetry can be taught. 'One is born with it. There's no other way.'

He wrote some Sufi *shayari* and began reciting verses at *mushairas*. He began writing poetry of protest when some of the young people he knew were killed in encounters. He then wrote poetry against violence, against Kashmiri separatism and its leaders, in the course of which he made many powerful enemies.

Militants threatened him with death. He lampooned someone in the state, whose name he wouldn't take, so memorably, he says, that he ended up spending two years in jail. 'They charged me with being a member of a terror group, Harkat-ul-Ansar. I told them, sir, I'm a Shia. How could a Shia be a member of an extremist Sunni outfit?' But the argument didn't work. In jail, he was frequently attacked by those whom he had outraged through verses such as this:

Aesi kya karun, aes kya karaan
Ze ze darjan dohoi maraan
Filhaal thaivtav bandook tulith
Jang karyiv amanuk jaam walith
[What's to be done, what are we doing
Dozens of people every day are dying
For now keep those guns at ease
Wage war but in the shroud of peace]

'Militants used to come up to me asking me to write rousing poems for Azadi, and their friends' obituaries. Some Shia spiritual leaders would come asking me to write *marsiyas*. I got tired of all of them. I asked them to go away. But they wouldn't.'

'Did you stop writing poetry then?'

'I didn't stop writing, I just stopped reciting it.'

I asked him to describe the events of the night when he lost his house, his library and all his verses.

It happened on 15 March 2018. Three armed militants barged into his house. 'They were young boys, quite exhausted. I told them, "You will die in the encounter. But you know what happens to the house of the person in which you die?" They said, "We are so exhausted we can't move an inch. Our death has brought us to your doorstep." For five hours, I pleaded with them to go away so that my house could be spared. But they refused to move. So, with my family, I stepped out.'

It was an old house, mainly built of stone. The forces which had surrounded the house kept shelling it, but it wouldn't fall. Then they poured some inflammable oil on it and set it on fire. 'I watched my house burn for twelve hours, through the night. I thought of going to someone's place to spend the night there. But my feet wouldn't take me away. Thirty years of my work were there in that house. And a library of around eight hundred books, some of which were quite rare.'

Did he try to look for his books?

'*Haan, main pehle udhar hi gaya, par kitna nadaan tha main . . . jahan taamba pighla hua tha main wahan kaaghaz dhuund raha tha* [Yes, that's where I first went, but how innocent I was . . . where copper had melted I was looking for paper].'

'My book's been burned?' Agha Shahid Ali wondered aloud in his poem 'Of Light'. 'Send me the ashes, so I can say: I've been sent the phoenix in a coffin of light.'

I tell him how I felt about his tragedy. That it seemed to be a fitting metaphor for the thirty-year-old conflict in Kashmir, among whose great casualties were the arts and culture. I couldn't think of the Urdu word for 'metaphor'. In its place I used '*misaal*', which in Urdu means 'an example'.

Balhami understood what I meant. 'It is true, what you're saying. But I'm not the only one. Many have suffered similar fates. It is also true that violence had the most destructive effect on culture. People used to invite singers to big events like weddings and festivals. But for the last twenty years I haven't heard anyone sing. That's because the tears haven't dried up yet. There are some poets still alive, but poets can only write what they see. But our poets cannot write what they see.'

Balhami recited from memory a few verses he had composed on the things he had seen in his life. 'There was a madman who lived not far from Balhama,' he said. 'He was shot by security forces who mistook him for a militant.' Balhama wrote this verse on his death:

Kochas manz os kustaam chor
Tas kya payi tem ked dor
Gool chalei tas fil for
Khosh gayi dahshatgard ha mor
[There was a loony in an alley dimly lit
What did he know, he made a dash for it
When they sprayed fire on him, he was hit.
They cheered. They had killed a terrorist]

Not everything Balhami had written was destroyed. After the news about his house spread, many friends and well-wishers stepped forward with copies of his work.

'There was a friend of mine. I didn't know this but he used to publish my poems every day on his Facebook page. He called to say he had some 120–150 pages with him. My readers had by themselves collected my verses . . . from memory, from words written on the last page of someone's notebook, which they sent to me. Another friend called to say that he had long ago borrowed a copy of my verses, so he had some fifty, sixty pages with him.'

And the rest?

'Thousands of young boys used to note down the poetry I recited in gatherings, at funerals. It lives there with them, in their handwriting.'

A few years ago, I had heard Hungarian novelist László Krasznahorkai describe a similar loss. In his barely audible, soft voice, he described how he had lost all his books in a fire that had engulfed his home, how the loss of his personal library had crushed him. Kurt Vonnegut, the great American satirist, in a letter written in November 2004, four years after his house, his books and all his papers were reduced to ashes, said, 'I have scarcely had a day worth living since the fire, am bored absolutely shitless by myself.'[1]

Balhami had a curious habit. After reciting some verses, he would often say, 'Ye badi sakht nazm hai [This verse is very severe]' and stop reading. What is so severe about them, I asked. Very well then, Balhami would say, and continue to read further. He recited many verses he had written in his youth, poems glorifying Kashmiris killed in gun battles, and the idea of 'Azadi'. And some verses mocking separatists. Through this he also answered a question I had asked at the beginning of our interview, on why he did not want to publish his work. 'This is why I don't want to get published. If I publish these nazms do you think I'll live for another day?' There was little to argue with that.

'Mad Ireland hurt you into poetry,' W.H. Auden wrote in his farewell to W.B. Yeats.[2] 'Now Ireland has her madness and her weather still.' Balhami is condemned not just to writing verses in a similar atmosphere of conflict, but to never seeing his verses in print. If there is a consolation, it is in knowing that there will always be somebody, a one-time audience member perhaps, in whose mind at least a few lines of Balhami will keep resonating. Auden continued: 'For poetry makes nothing happen: it survives . . . A way of happening, a mouth.'

Would he consider getting published posthumously? 'Yes, that could be the only way.' When asked what he would like to call his posthumous collection, Balhami thinks for a while before responding. '*Aesi kya karun, aes kya karaan* [What's to be done, what are we doing?]. Yes, this seems to be appropriate. This is what I'll name my book.'

Balhami is a restless man. When he's not speaking, he doesn't hide the impatience with which he sometimes looks at his feet, sometimes at the ceiling. But after a few hours with him, it doesn't bother me any more.

'*Mujhe hi dekh lo. Darasal shayar ka koi mazhab nahi hota. Lekin Hindustan ki fauj ne mujhe maar maar ke Mussalmaan bana diya* [Actually, a poet doesn't belong to any faith as such. But Indian forces beat me into becoming a Muslim].' He feels that the Indian government's biggest failure in Kashmir is that it went to war with the same people it called its own. 'They always treated us like a bunch of villains. Kashmir is not Afghanistan. Give us love and we'll love you back. But India has responded to this political issue with bullets.'

Balhami once made a pilgrimage to Mirza Ghalib's tomb in Delhi. 'I went all the way down to see Ghalib's tomb and found a goat tied outside it. It was terrible. I couldn't bear it. I returned home immediately.' Now he wants to die peacefully in Kashmir. 'But I fear one day someone will find a nazm of mine and get really angry. Times are changing, you see. I have seen a lot of people die.

I feel a stray bullet will hit me one day and that will be that. I wrote a nazm about it. Do you want to hear it?'

Dilli waalon tumhari sangdilli par
Main to rounga cheekhunga chillaunga
Islamabad tumhari bedilli ke bhi marsiye
Likh likh ke logon ko sunaaunga
Fir na jaane kis bandook ki goli se
Main yunhi maara jaaunga
[O the rulers of Delhi on your cruelty
I'll wail and shout and cry hoarse
O the rulers of Islamabad on your savagery
I'll write reams and recite them in public of course
Then, who knows! Whose gun will fire the bullet
That will silence me perforce]

'*Aage ki nazm badi sakht hai. Abhi itna hi kaafi hai* [The verses that follow are quite severe. This should do for now].'

5

The Old Man of Shopian

I got my first serious bit of advice on writing from my maternal grandfather. It was about looking up, rather than guessing, the meanings of words. More than twenty years ago, during my summer holidays, which I used to spend at his home in Jammu, I showed him a stack of my poems. I wished to be a poet then.

He took a very keen interest in what I had written. That was how he was towards children, indulgent and encouraging. After a few moments of silence, he put down my notebook and remarked upon my inexact use of a word. 'Solitude and loneliness are very different emotions. Don't mix them up. Loneliness is hurtful. Solitude is when you're happy by yourself,' he said, simplifying it for my benefit. Now that he had pointed out the difference, I wondered if he had ever felt either of them. 'Yes, I feel a bit of both each day,' he said.

For the next many days, I observed him, but it was hard to tell whether he was sad or at peace with himself. Omkar Nath Seru was a proud man and a high-ranking bureaucrat in his time. After his retirement, he spent his hours—as did my paternal grandfather, as I suppose all retired people do—in bringing order to the things and people around him. But there was still a lot of spare time and he spent it on missing home. You could tell, for instance, by the thoroughness with which he read the obituaries section of *Daily Excelsior* every day, just like his fellow Jammu-based exiles, looking for familiar names and faces. When he was not reading obituaries, he spent his time relishing Charles Dickens and Thomas Hardy. Missing home meant oscillating between loneliness and solitude while keeping one's feelings strictly private, especially from the prying eyes of children.

Many years later, I was reminded of that distinction when I visited the house of Omkar Nath Bhat. He was in an even stranger place mentally than my grandfather, who died far away from his home. Bhat hadn't left his home, but was still at a great remove from it. He lived in a place called Hal in south Kashmir's Shopian. It used to be a thriving neighbourhood of at least a hundred Pandit families. Today it is a ghost town. Only one family lives there, that of Omkar Nath Bhat's. I distinctly remember the dread I felt when I first saw Hal.

You'll find it on the Pulwama–Srinagar road, on the right, if you're driving towards Srinagar. Its large brick houses, with tin roofs and wooden beams, are still in a state of collapse thirty years after they were abandoned. A thick coat of green is closing in on them. Weeds are making their way in through the front entrances. Some of those entrances were once adorned with intricate wood carvings and colourful stones, which have retained their shapes, if not their colours, despite the blows of nature and time. A few walls bear faint outlines of the swastika. There are houses with crumbling upper floors that look like headless phantoms. Alleys between closely built houses are run over by nettles.

While wandering in these ruins two years ago, I heard faint noises from a house that, from the outside, looked as deserted as the others. I walked towards it, and on finding a Pandit family living there, felt a heady mix of joy and relief. It was like finding a heaving chest in a scatter of lifeless bodies.

I was standing outside the faded blue door of his house again in the summer of 2019. With all the energy that the frail eighty-two-year-old man could summon, Bhat shouted, 'Come in.' Just like that, without even seeing my face.

The last time I had knocked, his wife had opened the door. The inner walls of his house had a thick coat of mud. This is how, before the time of electric radiators, people insulated their rooms against the severe cold. We walked up to his room on the first floor, which faced the front of the house. 'What did you say your name was, again?' he asked. I told him. 'Wait,' he said and reached out for an old business diary on a shelf above his head. It was kept next to a dysfunctional radio that he had bought some forty years ago. 'This?' he asked, pointing at a page in the diary where I had written my name and phone number. He remembered!

The pink walls of his room were covered with images of Hindu gods. There was Shankar, the most revered god of Kashmiri Pandits, Parvati, and Ganesh, and Guru Nanak too. On the other side of the room, near the door, was a small bed and a black-and-white television set. With his cropped white hair, high cheekbones, large nose and thin frame, Bhat looked quite like the old Samuel Beckett. He called out to his daughter-in-law for tea, but not hearing from her, got up and returned with some bananas. That was all he had to offer, he said.

I saw his wife's photo hung on the wall just over his head. 'Yes, she died two months ago.' He finished the fruit and turned his head towards the window on his right. This was exactly how I remembered him—seated on a worn-out carpet with a cushion supporting his back, looking out of the window into the distance.

Which did Bhat feel more acutely, I wondered, solitude or loneliness? He lived in a setting that Pandits who had fled to faraway lands would consider their worst nightmare. The exiled Pandits could look away, their children could forget and their grandchildren could begin afresh. But he could see—and he did see, every waking hour—the remains of lives that were once intimately entwined with his own. As could his grandson who had scratched his name out on the faded blue door.

'This one,' Bhat said, pointing to the collapsed structure in front of his house, 'is where lived the Khans. Those two houses over there were homes of the Vaishnavis.' Another pile of debris was the house of the Panditas, that one there belonged to the Bhats, near them lived the Reshis, Halis, Punjabis, Mallahs, Kauls and so many more.

'There was no shortage of anything. The butcher was there, milk was in abundance. Herath used to be such a huge event. Muslims would come and offer to cook fish for us. We used to celebrate each other's festivals. It used to be a very noisy place back then.'

The memories of his childhood and youth were filled with the sounds of celebration. He remembered them fondly.

'I have this memory from a time when I was a very young child. My friend and I were walking along Amira Kadal. The entire Srinagar was adorned with bunting. We also stood with the public to see the spectacle. It was a *dariyai juluus* [a river procession, which was quite commonly carried out in Jhelum in those days]. There were lots of people in Jhelum and out on the roads. Everyone was excited. It was only through the local papers the next day that we found that the juluus was for Gandhi. He had come to Kashmir.'

Mahatma Gandhi is said to have visited Kashmir only once, in the first week of August 1947. Noted historian Ramachandra Guha remarks that when Gandhi reached the valley, 'he received a terrific reception. On his entry into Srinagar he was met by thousands of people on either side of the road, shouting "Mahatma Gandhi *ki jai*". Since the bridge across the Jhelum river had been taken over by the crowd, Gandhi took a boat to the other side, where he addressed a public meeting of some 25,000 people, convened by Sheikh Abdullah's wife. He spoke of spiritual rather than political matters, in Hindustani. His doctor, Sushila Nayar, who was with him, wrote that 'men and women flocked from the neighbouring villages to have a glimpse of the Mahatma. Friends and foes alike wonder at the hold he has on the masses. His mere presence seems to soothe them in [a] strange fashion'.[1]

This was nearly seventy-two years ago, and Bhat would have been a ten-year-old boy at the time. But he still remembers what his friends, who had heard Gandhi speak, told him about the speech. 'Yes, it was sort of spiritual,' he said.

'Gandhi in his speech said that the people of Kashmir are very poor. They needed to be brought at par with the rest. He said that the Kashmiri man was so broke he could not even afford a *langot* [loincloth],' he said, breaking into laughter like a school child. His version of Gandhi's speech sounded slightly dubious, but there was something about how he said 'langot' that left us both shaking with laughter for the next several minutes.

Into this *dariya* several years later, he would almost drown.

'I used to work in SP High School [Srinagar] then, before I moved to the horticulture department. Our working hours were from 7 a.m. to 1 p.m. In the summers, it used to get terribly hot in the afternoons. We used to go to Raghunath Mandir to swim after office. My problem was, although I could swim, I didn't know how to make a U-turn, you see. So one day I dared myself and tried to turn around when all of a sudden I started drowning. I mean I actually was drowning. I could feel my feet touch the floor of the river. But my friends came and saved me. A crowd had gathered on one side of the bank. The first thought that came to me after I was pulled out was that someone from that crowd was going to inform my parents. I feared getting thrashed at home.'

Did he get thrashed?

'Oh yes. I was beaten black and blue that day.'

Then what happened?

'Then everyone started leaving.'

Why?

'People started receiving threats. We knew that those people weren't bluffing. Everyone became sad and quiet.

'The conversations between us [Kashmiri Pandits] reduced over the next few days. Till one day when we altogether stopped speaking to each other. All of us were alone in those moments. One day we saw locks hanging on one house. The next day we saw locks hanging on more houses. Soon, throughout Hal, there were locks everywhere. Nobody told us when they were going. People just quietly left.'

Why didn't he leave?

'We wanted to. But we did not have the means. Where could we have gone? As days and a few months passed, I decided if we had to die, it was better to die here, on our own soil.'

Did he write anything? Make notes? What a witness he had been!

'No . . . Actually, I had started to keep a diary, but my son advised me against it. I saw everything but kept my mouth shut.'

~

There was, however, one Kashmiri who did keep a diary of those dark times and wrote movingly as he saw his friends, his favourite haunts and his culture wither and fade away—Agha Shahid Ali. He was by far the most talented Kashmiri poet in the English language. An admirer of Begum Akhtar, Lorca, Cavafy, Iqbal and Faiz. He was the voice of the hurt and despairing Kashmiri.

After being introduced to his collection *Veiled Suite* by a friend a few years ago, I spent most of my time memorizing lines such as this:

For I had also seen the moth rush to the candle—
then nothing but the wrenched flame gasping in knots.[2]

I also began imitating his way of seeing things—arms that were 'turquoise with veins', guns that were 'punctual stars', a heart that was 'still unbriefed, but briefly lit'. Briefly lit. That's how the world looked like in his pages.

> Just promise him the rain/ and pour wine into his glass/ His veins illuminated/ his blood is ink/ He's writing the world's sorrow ('From Another Desert')
>
> I never swear, but . . . notice the thinness/ of breaths about to break. We recycle/ them wholly black till their cobwebs incandesce ('A Fate's Brief Memoir')
>
> On these beaches/ the sea throws itself down, in flames/ as we bring back, at sunset, the incarnadine of light ('Of Light')
>
> Of course, I'll say something about the Taj Mahal/ silvering in the moonlight all week in marble ('In Marble')

Light was also the motif of 'I See Kashmir from New Delhi at Midnight', a poem that taught me a great deal about how fundamentally different, and at odds with each other, were our stories of pain. We, Pandits and Muslims, could bond over so many things—music, our shared language, and its inherently dry state of humour. But our tragedies were irreconcilable.

That poem had some unforgettable lines:[3]

> The city from where no news can come
> is now so visible in its curfewed night
> that the worst is precise:
> From Zero Bridge
> a shadow chased by searchlights is running
> Away to find its body.

And then Agha Shahid Ali went on to say:

> By that dazzling light
> we see men removing statues from temples.

We beg them, 'Who will protect us if you leave?'
They don't answer, they just disappear
on the road to the plains, clutching their gods.

It was incredible that the only thing that someone as sensitive and
as observant as him saw was the Pandits leaving. He didn't notice
the systematic hate campaign, or the ethnic violence against them.
An entire community was on the run right in front of his eyes and
the one question he had for them was: Why don't you stay and
protect us! Shahid never asked them why they left. Not once.

'They don't answer, they just disappear'. In his memoir *Our
Moon Has Blood Clots*, Rahul Pandita quotes a few[4] verses written
by the poet Maharaj Krishan Santoshi for his friend Naveen Sapru,
who was brutally killed in Srinagar's Habba Kadal in February
1990.

Naveen was my friend
Killed he was, in Habba Kadal
while on the tailor's hanger remained hung
his warm coat.
Passing as it did through scissors and threat-needle
in the tailor's hand, till the previous day
it was merely a person's coat
that suddenly was turned into a Hindu's coat

If Shahid couldn't see it, few others could. Through another poem,
Farewell,[5] he wrote a letter to a Kashmiri Pandit. He began it
with a caveat: 'At a certain point I lost track of you.' The Pandit,
he lamented, meanwhile, had turned him, that is, the Kashmiri
Muslim, into an enemy. He heard nothing else from the displaced
Pandit. Shahid, that is, the Kashmiri Muslim, 'hid the pain even
from myself'. If at all he heard the Pandit's pain—his brutalization,
his days in a ramshackle relief camp—he never mentioned it.
Again, he had drawn a line. Again, he found himself on the right
side of it.

In your absence you polished me into the Enemy.
Your history gets in the way of my memory.
I am everything you lost. You can't forgive me.
I am everything you lost. Your perfect enemy

He was the voice of the despairing Kashmiri, but that voice was not mine. Not always. 'Shahid', as he tells us in a poem, means a witness in Arabic. In his case it was also a gift. Which is why it hurt that of such a great tragedy, which also unfolded before him, he just made footnotes.

~

Somewhere near Srinagar, I had a long chat with a Kashmiri Pandit woman who had returned a few years ago to the valley after being given a government job. She recalled the months following July 2016 when mobs had gone on a rampage, angry with the killing of Hizbul Mujahideen commander Burhan Wani. I had written from Kashmir, a year after that encounter, about how Pandits were living in fear after some of their transit camps were attacked by the mobs.

'For weeks, my daughter and I could not step out. We could hear gunshots almost every other day. But our Muslim neighbours were generous. They did not let us remain hungry for a day even. They brought us daily groceries and got us a cab out as soon as there was a pause in the violence.'

But that was not the only time she and her daughter had felt threatened. 'We had once gone to visit a nearby temple sometime in 2017. While we were returning, some local boys threw stones at our car. My daughter, who was six years old then, never quite recovered from that fright. One day she told me that her classmates had said something about her identity. Come what may, she said, she wouldn't live for another day in Kashmir. A phobia caught hold of her. I couldn't lose my job, so I had to leave her with my mother in Jammu, where she stays to this day.'

Just then she got a call from her daughter, who was looking for her socks. Sunita* told her where to find them.

'Wednesdays they have a different uniform, you see. My daughter is quite lonely without me. She can't sleep unless I sing to her on a video call. The times when the Internet is shut for long durations, it really takes a toll on her. She gets panicked by little things.'

Sunita says she sees the same phobia, the same fear, in the eyes of the local Muslim children she teaches.

'I can see that their careers are getting destroyed. As a teacher it pains me but there is nothing I can do. This fear is like a drug. It eats these children from inside. Some of these children face a lot on the streets also. How much will you punish them?—I think sometimes when I look at the photos of their bruised, battered bodies.'

I ask her how different Kashmir is in reality as opposed to the mental picture that most people, living thousands of miles away, have in their minds.

'The television debates, I think, are not really helping. The reality here is much more complex. There are people who will go out of their way to make you feel at home. But then there is also a whole new generation of kids who don't even know who Pandits are, who have never ever met a Pandit.'

Despite everything, she doesn't want to leave Kashmir. She will stay put because it reminds her of a beautiful past, because she feels that she shouldn't have to flee her home again.

'*Sochti hun ki nikal jaun lekin fir lagta hai main apni jagah hun. Main fir nahi niklungi. Main displaced nahi hun* [I think of leaving sometimes but then I feel that I'm home. I won't leave again. I am not yet displaced].'

In *The Enigma of Arrival*, V.S. Naipaul[6] looks back at his time in a cottage which he had once lived in, when he wasn't sure how long he'd last.

---

* Name changed to protect her identity.

After that first spring I would say: 'At least I had a spring here.'
And then I said: 'At least, I had a spring and summer here.'
And: 'At least I've had a year here.' And so it went on, as the
years passed. Until time began to telescope, and experience
itself began to change: the new season not truly new anymore,
bringing less of new experience than reminders of the old.
One had begun to stack away the years, to count them, to take
pleasure in the counting, the accumulation.

A LONG WALK WITH
THE BAKARWALS

On the day we were supposed to meet, the Bakarwal called up. His family had changed their mind. They were leaving without me. I had been planning this journey with him for the past three months. And it was already mid-September, the peak season for the migration of Bakarwal nomadic shepherds from Kashmir to Jammu. To make things absolutely clear, he switched off his phone. But this was no time to panic. I needed to find another Bakarwal host as soon as possible. I roped in a couple of friends.

We came across some families in Chattergul in Anantnag. The three of us confidently approached a family that was camping in a lush green meadow. We asked how they felt about accommodating an extra traveller. Without any formalities, we were told to push off.

We then approached the headman of another Bakarwal family. We were destined to meet, my friends and I argued tactfully, for what else could bring us, creatures of two different worlds, together in this unlikely place? The old Bakarwal, who sported a long white beard, had a weather-beaten face and a Buddha-like calmness about him. He asked us to sit down. There we stayed for nearly half an hour, staring at him as he tended to his sheep and told us about his life. In the end, he decided it was better that we returned the following year.

Trying not to lose heart, we made our way towards another Bakarwal family that had pitched tent lower down the hill. We were offered tea and some favourable news. The family chief told us he was planning on resuming their journey in the next couple of days. He had no problem taking me along. 'So, should we get his stuff?' my friends asked in the manner of sealing the deal. 'Oh,' he said, as if he'd suddenly remembered something, 'Give me a minute.' Five minutes later, he said his family would actually stay where they were for another ten days. It was a polite refusal.

With no other Bakarwal left to chase, we started heading back towards our car. On the way, we met a shepherd who told us about a group of Bakarwals who were resting on top of a hill in Ganderbal. They had left Gurez a week ago, he said. They could start off on their journey at any moment. We reached the spot slightly after 2 p.m.

It was a hill overlooking Srinagar. A female voice from inside a tent directed us to where the senior Bakarwal men were sitting together, soaking in the sun. We introduced ourselves. My friend opened the conversation with a moving—and not entirely dishonest—monologue on the miseries afflicting Bakarwals. '*Sahi baat* [Rightly said],' said one of the men. With this little encouragement, my friend then launched into a full-blown sermon on the unjust social realities that had arrested the progress of this nomadic tribe. He rounded off his speech with a warning— unless someone were to travel with them, live as they did, eat what they ate and write about it all, the state and its people would never realize their plight. '*Sahi baat*,' said the same man again.

'When do you leave?' my friend asked the Bakarwal.

'Tomorrow.'

'Great. So we'll get his stuff then?'

'Sure.'

'Run for it before he changes his mind,' one of my friends whispered to the other.

Within ten minutes, I was standing outside the Bakarwal tent alone with my bags. Before allowing me in, the man, who introduced himself as Mohammed Nazeer, put forth a condition: if I were to fall ill or injure myself, I would be on my own. Neither he nor his family would waste their time on me. I agreed, and just like that became a part of his caravan.

I walked over to the tent not knowing what I should do. Could I read? Would it be appropriate to start taking notes? Should I perhaps observe them for some time? Help them with their chores? To seem occupied, I began unpacking and packing things while getting a better look at the tent that was going to be my home for the next few days. It was about 10 feet by 7 feet in size. At the back of it was a heap of blankets. On my left some chopped wood and to the right some basic utensils—a couple of unwashed plastic cups, a pot, some plates. This was the home of Nazeer's younger brother, Riyaz, his wife, Raziya Begum, and their three children. I would be making my bed here along with them, in the little space that was left by the firewood. Seven such tents were pitched close to each other on that hill.

At about 3.30 pm, a woman began to cook chapattis at the entrance of the tent. On a small wrought iron frame—two conjoined circles supported by four legs—she was making what in Kashmir is called *sheer chai* or *noon chai*, a pink, salty tea. I was offered a chapatti with a cup of tea.

I had brought along with me a copy of Rebecca West's *Black Lamb and Grey Falcon*. I sat down with it. A few pages in, a child who had been observing me came closer. He asked what I was reading. Curtly, I told him that it was a book.

'What is it about?'

This was a complicated question. The book is West's first-person travel account to Yugoslavia published in 1941, around the time of its invasion by the Nazis. It's about the thrill of coming across the terrifying desolation of Kosovo, the scattered lights of Sarajevo, the sculpted beauty of Macedonia. As well as about the conflicting histories of the Balkans, the rise of fascism, and the premonition of the Second World War. But how could I, to begin with, explain to this boy the idea of a nation? Or, what was even worse, a former nation?

'It's about a country,' I said, using the Urdu word '*mulk*' while outlining an imaginary big ball to suggest vastness.

'Which country?'

'Yugoslavia.'

'Yugo,' he half repeated, taking the book from my hands. A youth entered the tent at that moment to introduce himself. '*Tu bohot gora chitta hai. Aise to log tujhe alag se pehchaan jaayenge. Magar tu chinta mat kar. Do-teen din mein hum tujhe pura Bakarwal bana denge* [You're very spic and span. Anyone will be able to tell you apart. But don't worry, within a couple of days we'll turn you into one of us].'

Around dusk, when it got too dark to read, I stepped out of the tent. From a nearby hill, shepherds were descending with hundreds of goats and sheep. All I could see were their silhouettes. They didn't seem to be in any hurry. Cups of tea and chapattis were taken to the men as the shepherds counted their flock. Nothing was amiss. Half an hour later, we all had dinner. Nazeer came to the tent with a torch that he held to my face. He had come to check on me. Everything was in order, I said, wincing back from the blinding torchlight. I could sense some movement behind him. More people had followed him into the tent.

'*Nasha karta hai*?' he asked me. 'Do you drink or smoke?' He had a naturally booming voice. I couldn't help but notice that the light on my face and the tenor of that question were giving our conversation shades of professional interrogation.

'*Nahi* [No],' I said, smiling.

'*Kahan rehta hai* [Where do you live]?'

'*Dilli mein* [In Delhi].'

'*Ghar bech diya yahan* [Have you sold your house here]?'

'*Haan* [Yes].'

'*Yahan koi rishtedaar nahi* [You don't have a relative here]?'

'*Nahi* [No].'

He paused.

' *Pandit hai* [Are you a Pandit]?'

'*Haan* [Yes].'

'*Ye Pandit hai* [He's a Pandit]!' Nazeer declared loudly with an air of triumph. I hadn't told them this fact when we first met. It wasn't part of a carefully laid-out plan. I just didn't like being the subject of everyone's inquiry. Also, to be honest, I wasn't really sure how they would take it.

I waited for Nazeer's reaction. The eyes of all the men of his caravan were on him. I could also sense heads shift to get a better view of me. For a lot of them, the younger ones especially, I may have been the first Kashmiri Pandit they were meeting.

'*Jaise hamare yahan pir hote hain na, inke yahan Pandit hote hain* [Like we have pirs in our community, they (Hindus) have Pandits],' Nazeer told his audience with a smile. It felt like a sign of approval. Following their masters, some goats had also entered the tent and joined the conference.

'*Tu nasha nahi karta na* [You don't drink or smoke, no]?' Nazeer asked again.

'*Nahi* [No].'

'*Main bhi nahi karta* [Nor do I],' he said, laughing, and slapped me on the shoulders with such force that I could sense a ripple of shock travel down the spine. All along, the little boy who wanted to discuss the book kept staring at me blankly.

Nazeer asked me to teach Urdu to all the children in the caravan. I didn't know Urdu, I said, but I could teach them some English. And a little Hindi, if they wanted.

'English,' the little boy repeated with a smile. His name was Rashid. He was Nazeer's son.

Everyone followed Nazeer out of the tent. Riyaz and his family made their beds and prepared to sleep. I unrolled my sleeping bag. My first day with them had come to an end and I was quite unsure what I had gotten myself into.

We woke up at 6 a.m. the next morning. It had rained through the night, and all night long a child had wailed in a nearby tent. In the morning when I stepped out of the tent, I found the whole of Srinagar at my feet.

I hadn't realized the beauty of the place till then. Before us, the vast sky, heavy with thick, dark clouds, hung over Srinagar. Somewhere in the middle was Hari Parbat, surrounded by the densely packed old city, the downtown. To our left was the Dal. Coiled around it like a snake was the shining boulevard. Directly below were rich green golf courses, which hadn't lost their colour despite the onset of autumn. Far, far behind them all, on the horizon, sat the imperious, white Pir Panjal mountains. On the other side of them was Jammu. Very soon, we would have to climb one of those peaks. To our distant right was a peak on which three bright dots appeared every night. Nazeer told me later that this was Gulmarg. After dusk, Srinagar sparkled like a cluster of fireflies.

I looked around and absorbed the commune in which I was living. There were about a dozen horses, some 500 sheep and goats, seven tents, and close to thirty people. I had heard stories back home about how Bakarwal women liked to wear a lot of silver. Out here everyone was in tatters. Women and young girls wore the salwaar kameez which, when they were not cooking or feeding their children or balancing large pots of water on their heads, they would work on with colourful threads. Apart from the routine wear and tear, little shooting flames from makeshift stoves kept poking holes in their clothes. The women would keep fixing them till their clothes looked like Kandinsky's canvases. The men, too, wore simple, worn-out kurta pyjamas.

The three senior-most figures, the ones with shaved heads (which, it turns out, is a now out-of-fashion style for Bakarwal men)—Nazeer, and his two older brothers, Majeed and Kaka—also wore turbans made of small towels. Some of the men carried sticks, mostly to keep straying sheep and goats in line. Only Majeed walked around with a proper staff. He was also the only man in the commune wedded to two women.

The idea of having two wives didn't seem to appeal to any other man here. I heard that the white-bearded hermit, Kaka, who had spent forty years of married life without an offspring, had once toyed with the idea but dropped it later. He had perhaps found joy in other things—like smoking bidis. Kaka was the only person here who could smoke around Majeed, in whose towering presence everyone, including the goats, behaved themselves.

Shortly after the morning tea, three local butchers reached Nazeer's tent to buy goats. After half an hour of intense bargaining, he sold them five goats for Rs 30,000. 'You see the losses we're making out here. I just sold five of my best goats for a pittance. When you go back to Delhi tell those people what wonderful goats we have. Tell the government in Delhi to buy goats only from us,' Nazeer said.

The Bakarwals had meant to resume their journey that morning. But the rains had delayed their plans. The excitement of packing up and moving ebbed and the day passed off uneventfully.

The next day, over the cup of evening tea, we resumed our conversation.

'How long have you been roaming like this?' Nazeer's wife, Koka, asked me. I gave her an arbitrary figure. 'How long will you continue doing this before you settle down?' she asked again. These were the questions I wanted to ask them, I told Koka.

Nazeer intervened before Koka could ask more questions.

'Everyone works to feed their families. Why are we here, suffering so much? For this,' he answered his own question by pointing at his belly. 'That's why he's also here. Isn't it?' he asked me. It wasn't strictly true. But the idea of telling them that I hadn't come here 'for this' felt obscene. So 'of course, of course' is what I said.

At around 7 p.m. they started packing their tents into small bundles. Within an hour we were ready. But at 11, a couple of hours before we were supposed to leave, a series of thunderclaps ripped the sky. It poured, then it rained, then it lashed. I hid under a tarpaulin which the women had quickly pulled up and made into a tent again. An hour later, a proper storm hit us, threatening to blow us off the hill along with all of our belongings. Gusts of icy winds were pushing the wooden sticks supporting the tent closer and closer to the ground.

It was so cold that I couldn't get up to unroll the sleeping bag or put on warm clothes. I just lay there half expecting to be mummified by dawn. With painstaking effort I checked the time. It was still 2 a.m. I couldn't move around to check on anyone. Was anyone else awake? Or had they all quietly left?

A last song then, I said to myself. I put on the earphones and switched on the radio in my phone. But I couldn't find any music. Couldn't there be a radio station which, say, played only final requests?

I don't know how I survived and when I slept. But I did wake up to see another morning. It was still overcast. There was no chance of us moving anywhere. Outside their tents, everyone went about their jobs as usual. I washed up, had breakfast and slept again.

~

'*Pahad pe chalega* [Will you come up the mountains]?' Nazeer's eight-year-old son, Rashid, woke me up to ask. There were three other children with him. I had been at Riyaz's tent ever since I came here and had not had a proper conversation with anyone till then. So yes, why not.

In a few minutes, five of us, including Rashid and his cousin Shakil, who must have been around sixteen, were ready to go. I had exchanged a few pleasantries with Shakil on the first day. He had two unique characteristics—an immense love for the double entendre and constant tremors throughout his body.

We started our trek up the mountain. I hadn't walked 10 feet before sheepdogs started barking at me. There were four of them, quite fierce-looking and easily provoked. They had made the job of answering nature's calls quite difficult, more so at night when it was harder to spot their dark fur.

About a kilometre up the mountain we came across a huge apple orchard on one side of the road. All of us were hungry.

We considered our options. Rashid was for plucking the apples hanging from boughs leaning out of the boundary wall. 'How can they be his? They're almost on the road,' he argued. It was a reasonable point of view but one that the owner of the orchard was unlikely to appreciate. After some deliberation, Shakil decided to make a formal request for the apples.

He returned loaded. We savoured them while walking as far as the road would take us. On the way back, Shakil gave me an extra apple from his quota. This was a sort of compensation for becoming the butt of his jokes, which, since he delivered them in his native Gojri language, were hard to understand. By the manner in which his audience kept falling all over the place, pointing their little fingers at me, I could tell that he was very good.

A few metres down the road, sensing his opportunity, Rashid came up to me while others raced ahead. '*Tu tension mat le. Koi kuch bole to mujhe batana* [Don't you worry. If anyone says anything to you, let me know].' After we walked a few paces together, he said, '*Yaar ye phone mujhe de dena jab hamare ghar pohonchega. Kisiko batana nahi. Hamari dosti tuut jaayegi nahi to. Theek hai na? Tu bilkul tension mat lena. Main hun na yahan.* [Just give your phone to me when we reach our home. Don't tell anyone. Otherwise our friendship will end. Fine? Don't you worry. I'm here for you].' The pint-sized, enterprising Bakarwal had just offered me protection in exchange for my mobile phone. Bakarwals, I found, are quite adept at bartering. '*Sauda karega* [Want to trade]?' is how I found Bakarwal men greeting perfect strangers.

We spent that night staring at the sky, looking for signs of a clearing, of an unclouded moon. But the moon appeared only as a faint white blur. All of us, Shakil, Rashid and the rest of the children, sprawled across the damp hill, gazed at the moon till we went to sleep.

There is an interesting account in West's travelogue of how she found out about the assassination of the king of Yugoslavia.[1]

She was tuning the radio to listen to some music while recovering from an operation. She 'turned the wrong knob and found music of a kind other than I sought, the music that is above earth, that lives in the thunderclouds and rolls in the human ears and sometimes deafens them without betraying the path of its melodic line. I heard the announcer relate how the King of Yugoslavia had been assassinated in the streets of Marseille that morning.'

A few sentences later, she continues:

> So I imagined myself widowed and childless, which was another instance of the archaic outlook of the unconscious, for I knew that in the next war we women would have scarcely any need to fear bereavement, since air raids unpreceded by declaration of war would send us and our loved ones to the next world in the breachless unity of scrambled eggs.
>
> That thought did not then occur to me, so I rang for my nurse, and when she came I cried to her, 'Switch on the telephone! I must speak to my husband at once. A most terrible thing has happened. The King of Yugoslavia has been assassinated.' 'Oh, dear!' she replied. 'Did you know him?' 'No,' I said. 'Then why,' she asked, 'do you think it's so terrible?'
>
> Her question made me remember that the word 'idiot' comes from a Greek root meaning private person.

I had become a very private person ever since I joined this group. I had also grown restless at the same time, thinking about the prospective adventures. But there wasn't much to do. I offered to chop wood for Koka and was quickly worn out. Balancing heavy pots of water on the head was clearly beyond me so I didn't even bring that up. Just as I didn't bring up the task of feeding the bloodthirsty hounds.

Rashid offered to take me to a couple of hilltops where shepherds would be served their lunches. When one stood near the tents facing Srinagar, the grassy patches of land, where the flock was taken for grazing, lay on hills to our right. From a distance, every morning and every evening, that's where a swarm of goats and sheep passed through a hole in the fence like osmosis. In a spirit of tradition, each year, the Bakarwals broke a portion of the fence. After their departure, this was mended by a local authority and it remained intact till the Bakarwals returned the following year. '*Oye! Tu theek hai na? Tu koi tension mat lena.*' Don't worry, Rashid said.

'*Dekh ke chal yaar, kya karta hai* [Look where you're stepping, man]?' Rashid scolded me repeatedly, asking me to walk on a path that only he could see. It took us two hours to climb up to deliver the food to Rashid's elder brother Saji and return to the base of the hill. Saji, given his thin figure, had a remarkable appetite. I rarely saw him not eating. He ate when he was on duty, returned to the tent to eat a pre-dinner meal as well as a post-dinner dinner.

On our way back, Rashid calmly asked what I thought was a well-meant question, '*Kuta khayega.*' The men had been talking about preparing meat that evening. This is what I thought he was now offering me. 'Kuta' must be meat in Gojri. '*Nahi* [No thanks],' I responded. A few seconds later he repeated his statement, as did I. Out of nowhere suddenly, two hounds started running towards me. Their final murderous leap was broken only at the last moment by Rashid's shouts. '*Maine bola tha. Kuta khayega* [I told you, dog will bite].'

We had again that evening packed all our belongings into bundles. It was cold but bearably so. Every family was huddled around their bonfires. Walking around, I found Altaf and Naseem sitting close to each other. They had been married for a year now. In the glow of that fire she looked happy, quite beautiful and at peace with herself. Altaf asked me to sit but I saw him tickle Naseem, who sprang up in playful delight each time. They needed to be left alone. I should have realized it earlier. I reached for the fire that the hermit, Kaka, had lit. His hut and his bonfire were always placed the farthest from everyone else's. He never spoke unless spoken to. I couldn't have asked for a better companion. Five hours later, at 3 a.m., we would begin the walk.

~

Kaka woke me up in time. The horses were being saddled and the flock was being rounded up. Everyone was shouting at everyone else. In the middle of the chaos, even as I rubbed my eyes, Nazeer asked whether I wanted to go with the horses or the sheep. '*Ghode ke saath jaayega ya bhed ke saath?*' I hadn't figured until that moment that the horses and sheep didn't travel together.

Majeed had started walking down the hill with the flock. There was no time to take a considered view of things. I left my rucksack with Nazeer, who agreed to load it on to a horse, and with my backpack rushed to catch up with Majeed. So it had started finally.

In half an hour, we had walked down the hill and were on the road. It felt as if walking with the shepherds, with grace and speed, came quite naturally to me. A minute later, I fell into a gutter, pushed by hundreds of marching goats and sheep to one side of the road and then off it. It was pitch-dark. Holding a torch and laughing hard, Shaheen came to my rescue.

I walked briskly to catch up with Majeed, one damp leg feeling significantly heavier than the other. He said that sheep and goats were scoundrels. 'Don't let them lead you,' he added. 'You lead them and always walk in the middle.'

Up on the hill, I didn't make much of them, but down here, the sheep and goats filled the bylanes that we walked on, causing a huge ruckus as they banged their heads on gates, knocked over garbage bins, and flattened metal roofing sheets used as fencing around small, private gardens. They were like a gang of skinheads returning from a football match—a match their team had lost, badly, on home turf.

Any moment now I expected an irate mob to descend upon us. Their fury would have burned brighter at seeing Shaheen and

Shakil run around, under cover of the din, knocking on front gates just for fun.

It took us another hour to leave behind the closely packed colonies and enter wider roads. It was still dark, though time for Fajr prayers. Wearing skull caps, men came from all directions, in pick-up trucks, scooters, cars and motorcycles. Azaans resounded all around us.

At a lecture, the recording of which is available online, Mukul Shivputra, son of the legendary Hindustani classical singer Pandit Kumar Gandharva and a musical genius himself, had recalled hearing a symphony of Azaans in Indore once.

He used to sing for the radio in Indore. For the recording he would come a day early and sleep at a Shani temple close to the radio station. One day he woke up early and heard the Azaans coming from all directions. He said it was like listening to a symphony. It was an experience, he said, he would never forget. He went on to make an interesting point about the music of the Azaan.

'*Azaan gaayi nahi jaati. Azaan kyunki dharm ki pukaar hai isliye wo gaayi nahi jaati. Dee jaati hai. Wo kewal ek pukaar hai. Aqeede vagarh gaaye jaate hain kyunki usmein 'Sa' establish ho jaata hai. Lekin Azaan mein nahi. Agar 'Sa' establish ho gaya to wo ghalat hai. Wo Azaan nahi hogi.*'

[Azaan is not sung. Because Azaan is the call of faith, it is not sung. It is delivered. It is only a call. Islamic hymns are sung because in them 'Sa' (the first note in Indian classical music) is established. Not in Azaan. If 'Sa' is established it is wrong. It won't be an Azaan], he said.

It was a little over 6 a.m. We had been walking for three hours now. The sun had still not come out. 'You tired?' Shakil asked. No, I wasn't. But I was worried about getting tired.

The Bakarwals had taken me along on the condition that the caravan wouldn't stop for me, no matter what. If I grew sick or tired or got hurt, I would be on my own. As we walked, still within the city limits, it was clear that exhaustion was the enemy I was likely to encounter first.

A day earlier, standing on the hill in front of our tent, Nazeer had tried to give me a sense of the distance we were to cover the next day. 'That hill, can you see? *Wooooo udhar* [Over there]. That's only as far as we can see. We will go much, much further than that tomorrow.' In trying to avoid the subject of physical exhaustion, my mind was focussing itself more sharply on it.

I realized that I could fret over wearing out midway through the journey. Or acknowledge that I was the only one in the caravan for whom the journey and the destination were almost the same thing. I was constantly reaching somewhere and starting something anew. All my companions had taken this trip many times. But for me, each moment was one I would almost certainly never live again. So what I needed perhaps was to remain suspended in the present continuous. Be at peace. Breathe in, breathe out. Feel the legs, like the second hand of the clock, go one-two, one-two, one-two, one-two . . .

'Are you tired yet?'

'No'.

I tried to focus the mind on other things. The events of the past twenty-four hours, for instance. Did anything stick out? Yes, an annoying boy.

It was around early one morning when I first saw him peep into my tent. I had heard a local family—husband, wife and their son—chatting with Majeed and his wife. Their tent was a few feet away from the one I was staying in. The man had come down to buy some goats, and had brought his wife and child along.

The wife wouldn't stop asking Majeed questions. Where had they come from, what did they eat, how much money did they make, how long were they going to be here, how many goats did they have? She also asked a question that I myself had been longing to ask but considered too personal, about Shakil's condition. Majeed told her that Shakil was about three years old when he fell from a tree. 'We took him to doctors in Jammu and Srinagar. We spent about Rs 3 lakh but his condition did not improve. It's all up to Him now.' Majeed, I imagined, must have pointed to the skies.

While the lady then started complaining about the lack of healthcare facilities in the state, her son drifted over from one side of my tent to another, and noticed me inside. I must certainly have come across as a curious object. Any other day I would have maybe smiled back at him. But at that moment, I was in no mood to be observed.

But observe me he did, for minutes on end, open-mouthed. I picked up my book and pretended to read. I could still sense him looking at me. I dropped the book and stared right back. The boy walked back to his mother. After a few seconds, I heard Majeed telling the woman that I was a journalist who was hitch-hiking with them, in order to write about them. Then the mother appeared at my tent. And the father. Then a volunteer from a local mosque on a fund-raising drive. Who told *him*? Was there a queue outside?

We were still walking in darkness. The clanging of goat and sheep bells were the only noises around us. What else could I turn my mind to?

Altaf's cousin Mushtaq, who must have been in his twenties, had come to me long after we had finished dinner, while everyone was still rolling their tents and personal effects into bundles before leaving the hill.

'*Mere bacche ye sab nahi karenge* [My children will not do this],' he had said.

It later occurred to me that he was confiding in me only because I was an outsider. Only in front of an outsider could he express emotions that would have appeared rebellious to those in the caravan.

Earlier that evening, I had asked youngsters, who were huddled around a fire, what plans they had for their future. Did any of them want to settle down? Did they want their children to join their caravan? Mushtaq had put up a typically boyish act at the time.

'The thing is I don't have a bride. Because I don't have a beard. See? First you tell me how to grow a beard, then I'll tell you what I'll do with my children,' he had said, clapping Altaf on the shoulder.

But here, away from his companions, Mushtaq sounded like a man on whom beard and thoughts had grown abundantly.

'I will settle down. This life is not worth living. We have some land. I will farm it and make ends meet.' He added, '*Aise to bacche khajjal ho jaayenge* [children will get spoilt like this].

'My father, my grandfather, my great-grandfather, everyone has been doing this back and forth. But it cannot go on like this. Unless I settle down in one place I will not be able to provide good education to my children.

'It's not as if we never went to school. Some of us did for some time. But then we were beaten at school. So we ran away. We were not encouraged to stay on. Rashid, Saji, they all went to school. They know the English alphabet. But like us, they also left the school and joined the caravan. My children will not run away from school. I won't let them.'

Dawn was beginning to break. In order not to draw the attention of the bystanders or the heavily armed forces to myself, I kept shuttling between Majeed, who was leading the flock, Shakil tottering in the middle, and Altaf and Shaheen at the back. I toyed with the idea of removing my glasses to blend in more with those I was travelling with, but thought the better of it.

Shortly after reaching Hazratbal, we came across the first batch of morning walkers. A sense of class shame was beginning to take over. Only three days ago, not very far from here, I had attended a close friend's wedding. In the course of sharing the meal and getting photographed, I had met people who could be marching down the road at that very moment. I continued to walk with my head down.

Looking at the morning walkers, Altaf asked me, 'Why do people in Srinagar walk in the morning?' Fresh air is good for the mind, I told him, just as exercise is good for the body. 'You fool,' Shakil said to Altaf, 'you don't know anything about these rich people. Girls in Srinagar are obese, rotund even. They walk to lose weight so that they can get married.'

With the flock dutifully scanning all the dustbins along the way, we marched past Hari Parbat into Rainawari, a locality in old Srinagar town which got its name from the Kashmiri Pandit Raina community. There is also a tale from Hindu folklore about how it got its name. Walter Roper Lawrence makes a reference to it in *The Valley of Kashmir* (1895).[2]

> Every educated Hindu and most Musalmans in Kashmir believe that the valley was once a vast lake on which the goddess Parvati sailed in a pleasure-boat from her mountain home on Haramak in the north to Konsa Nag lake in the south. In her honour the lake was known as Satisar, the tarn of the caste woman.

He goes on to refer to the folklore about a demon residing in the lake, who, after wreaking havoc for thousands of years, was challenged by Vishnu, along with Kashyap Rishi, the grandson of Brahma, when Vishnu struck the mountains of Baramulla and let out the waters of the lake. But when the water demon eluded Vishnu as well, Parvati dropped a mountain on him, finishing him off for good. That mountain was the Hari Parbat, and on it was built a shrine for Parvati. The area itself came to be known after Kashyap Rishi, the grandson of Brahma, who had first resolved to rid the valley of that demon.

'Are you tired yet?' Shakil asked a third time.

'No, Shakil. Why do you keep asking?'

'Because I'm tired.'

'Oh.'

'I can't do this. I'm hopping on to the next bus I find. You want to come along?'

'No. You go ahead. I'll follow on foot.'

It was about 7 a.m. when, walking through the streets of Rainawari, Shaheen and her young cousin shouted out a familiar name and ran towards a wall. It was the name of the eight-year-old Bakarwal girl who was drugged and gang-raped in a temple for a week, in January 2018, before being murdered.[3] Some people in Jammu had even marched in support of the rapists who were convicted by a trial court.[4] [5] Posters bearing her face, demanding justice, were put up all along the walls.

I did not feel it was the right time to ask Shaheen or the others about it. I don't think they wanted to talk about it either. Several days later, I brought the topic up with Majeed. He said he didn't know the family, or anyone else who did. It sounded like a lie. I tried to elicit from him some emotional response, approaching the subject in roundabout ways, but he offered nothing more than banal truisms about communal harmony. I dropped it.

The flock, meanwhile, was attracting a lot of attention. One by one, several butchers approached Majeed with offers that were quickly turned down. One hard-nosed negotiator kept walking in circles around Majeed, invoking his dead ancestors and every holy figure he could think of. Going by the jargon he threw at Majeed once in a while, making him silently nod in approval, the man clearly knew his meat.

Clean-shaven, thin-framed and well-dressed in a starched blue kurta, the butcher walked with us for a couple of kilometres from Rainawari to beyond Dal gate on the Srinagar–Leh highway. At this point, he finally cracked a deal for three goats.

I imagined him returning home that evening, boasting to his wife and children about his knack for the business and bemoaning the back-breaking work. And, as he licked his fingers clean of goat curry, leaving them all with some moral platitude about the need to work hard in life.

Srinagar was now behind us. Ahead lay Pampore, followed by Awantipora. My back was beginning to crack under pressure. I pleaded with Liyaqat, Nazeer's son-in-law, who was the same age as

Mushtaq, to carry my backpack. He didn't need much persuasion. He flung the bag around his shoulders as if it weighed nothing.

We had been walking for over six hours now. The sun was out. Our bellies were empty. I realized it wasn't just me who was feeling hungry when Shaheen, walking through downtown, playfully asked a baker for some bread. The baker shooed her away. Shaheen's younger cousin, barely ten, tried getting bread from another baker. She too returned empty-handed. One day, back at the camp, feeling slightly peckish, I had opened a small packet of dry fruits. A young boy spotted raisins. I offered him some. Chaos had broken out across the camp as children and adults tried to snatch dry fruits from each other. It had not occurred to me that the people I was walking with could not afford bread.

At around 2 p.m., we reached Awantipora. It was in a small clearing on the bank of a tributary of the Jhelum that we stopped. We spread out on a grassy patch, on the other side of which were lined several houses. A highway passed above us.

Nazeer, with his caravan of horses, on one of which was riding little Rashid, reached a few minutes later. Everyone started looking for food. The horses were unburdened. Only the essentials were taken out and in no time, we were eating our quota of half-cooked rice and unpeeled potatoes, which was going to be my diet for the entire trip. A few minutes later, the clean-shaven butcher returned with four other butchers. Majeed, slumped under a tree, signalled to his brothers to show them the inventory.

Sitting next to Majeed, I wondered how we—the lot of us, scratching our backs, surveying our feet, combing our dust-matted hair—would have looked to an outsider. I was clearly not beyond class shame yet.

From the alley in front of us, I heard a few noises. I saw Altaf and Rashid swinging from the low-hanging branch of a tree. Behind them, Shakil and Saji were standing in front of a boisterous little girl, who quite visibly came from an affluent family.

The girl, remarkably clean and well-dressed, had been on her cycle when she was stopped by the two boys. They were both guffawing while the little girl was screaming her head off. Shakil kept saying that he wouldn't let her pass and the girl kept threatening him with dire consequences. 'Shakil, let her go. We'll all get beaten up real bad,' I shouted. Shakil had a talent for inducing murderous rage in people. A few hours earlier, he had come close to being beaten up by the shopkeepers of Srinagar for shouting obscenities at them. Only a few minutes from now, he would jeer at a powerfully built passer-by. A day later, he would work up every member of the caravan in a state of frenzy by quietly slipping away into the woods. But somehow he always got away with it. Nobody ever touched him.

Tension was building on both sides. The little girl looked purposefully at Shakil and Saji, both of whom stared right back at her. Behind her was seated another little girl who clearly, like me, didn't want any trouble. Taking my cue perhaps, the first girl declared, 'If you don't let me go, you little punk, I'm going to get you beaten so bad . . .' Saji and Shakil blinked.

It was again time to leave. Everything had been packed and was being loaded on to the horses. Once again, I left a little early with the flock, Majeed shepherding us from the front.

Straight up the bridge and down on the other side we went, towards a strange noise. Its source was hidden behind trees and dust. It continued getting louder and reached its crescendo as we walked right into it, on a straight, cramped path with sloping sides. Dozens of stone-crushers that looked like giant mechanical spiders were working on both sides, screeching loudly as if giving birth to more stone-crushers.

We left the spider colonies for open fields. At about 4 p.m. we climbed back on to the highway. The heat, amplified by the metalled road and a shining steel fence, was toasting us stiff. Nobody remembered exactly when it happened, but at some point we had run out of water. Cars raced past only, it seemed, to rub it in. The occupants of these cars would often look at us in wonder. So many people were swishing past us in both directions, on so many spinning tyres that the highway sounded like a mountain spring.

After some time, we crossed over to the other side of the highway and walked down to an under-construction road. On both sides of the road stood tall poplars and shining silver birch trees.

While the flock was marching forth, Altaf suddenly changed course by 90 degrees to run towards a house on our left. Saji and Shakil followed him. They had spotted a hand-pump. Water, finally, after hours of walking in the hot sun. The lone arm of the hand-pump kept swinging up and down for the next several minutes.

The sun was about to set when we reached Pulwama. We became its central attraction. Soon we were surrounded by potential customers. Everyone started making inquiries. Barter inquiries were made first. Would they trade their biggest three goats for a mare? No. For a pony? No. A small horse? No. A small horse and two chickens? No. They were then replaced by parties with cash. But still no offer seemed to interest Majeed.

At an open ground, we finally unburdened our load. The men went to the far end where the flock had been gathered to take a headcount. This was to be our resting spot till the following morning. All the families quickly marked their spaces and prepared their kitchens. Six fires were up in no time. I hadn't looked forward to unpeeled potatoes and half-cooked rice with more relish in my life.

Suddenly, I saw Nazeer running with a torch in his hand. He said something to Majeed. Altaf and the old hermit were also with him. They were now running back to where the flock was gathered. Majeed began shouting at them. I asked him what had happened. 'Five sheep are missing. They stole it,' he said.

All the men were up and about now. The two Altafs, Jalal, Riyaz, Nazeer, Nisar and Shakil. They searched everywhere.

Somebody shouted for Liyaqat, who was married to Nazeer's daughter Rubina. Someone yelled back that Liyaqat had crossed the stadium-sized field and stepped into the adjoining village to look for the sheep. In the thick of the night all one could see were flashes of moving torch lights. The women and children waited for them. Nobody had touched their food.

The men returned after a long time, empty-handed. Nazeer came quietly, sat down and began chopping wood for the fire. He was distraught beyond measure. '*In hurramzaadon ne hamari paanch bhed chura li. Aap likhna apni diary mein* [The bastards stole five of our sheep. Do write this in your diary].' The theft had set them back by at least Rs 50,000. But none of the men talked about this at all. Everyone quietly went about having their dinners. Except the hermit.

Majeed told me that many years ago, Kaka, who used to be a solitary shepherd back then, was on a mountain when he was caught in a snowstorm. He was shepherding a flock of around forty. By chance, he found refuge in a cave where he also found space to fit in some goats and sheep. When the storm subsided after a few hours, he stepped out to find that all his flock tied outside had been stolen. He was left with a handful of goats and sheep. 'He used to be the angriest among us, the most ill-tempered. He once beat up a policeman in front of us. But that day, when he lost his sheep, and with them his life's investments, something in him changed permanently. He went quiet. And since that day he hasn't said much,' Majeed said. From a distance, the hermit, who saw us looking at him, smiled back as he smoked his bidi.

At the far end of the ground, Rashid was howling with anger. 'I will kill those sons of bitches. Damn them. I will tear them apart . . .' Nobody made any attempt to pacify little Rashid. He was the only one in the camp who gave voice to his anger. Tears rolled down his cheeks as he swore at ghostly figures. His sister Rabeena walked over with a small child in her arms and sat down next to

Rashid. He was exhausted now. He stopped howling and instead started to console his sister.

'I will set this right. Don't worry. I have some money, I'll collect more and we'll have enough to buy a small lamb. When that lamb grows it will give birth to more lambs, and we will recover our losses. Don't worry, Rabeena.'

Smudges left by the tears on his dusty face gave Rashid the appearance of a tiny guerrilla. It was getting darker and colder, and the camp fires were dying faster than fatigue could put us to sleep. I asked the hermit for a bidi. He gave me one and smiled. 'Well, such is life,' he seemed to say.

~

The next morning, I found myself cocooned in my sleeping bag, which was completely drenched in dew, as were my socks and shoes. It was around 6 a.m. and Nazeer was loading all their belongings in a truck. Others led by Majeed had already left with the herd. So the only option was to get inside the truck.

A choice had to be made between finding, in a bag bursting through its seams, a pair of dry socks, and taking the risk of wearing wet socks. Tired limbs reached out by themselves for the socks dripping with cold dew.

I decided to help Nazeer and the women with the load. On the ground were heaped gunny bags full of firewood, makeshift stoves, folded tents, clothes, blankets and food. Majeed's wife, Koka, asked me to pick up a bulging gunny bag. I tried my best but the bag wouldn't move. Altaf's wife was helping load the bags in the truck with her child tied to her back. I started to look for lighter stuff like saddles and bags of groceries. In half an hour, we were ready to leave. Except, nobody could find Shakil.

The two Altafs, Nazeer and the women scurried around shouting his name. Of all the people it was Shakil, the one with a shaky constitution and clouded mental faculties, who was missing, in a forest located in a very violent part of Kashmir, without a phone. Let's not forget, he couldn't read or write either.

The truck driver was getting impatient. Nazeer had to take a call. Majeed and the others with the flock would reach the designated spot on time. He asked us all to sit in the truck. Nazeer and I sat in the front while the remaining few goats, and all the women and children found their place at the back. We started driving slowly along the road as Nazeer tried to see if his son was somewhere in the jungles to our left.

I thought I saw something far in the distance behind the last row of trees, I told Nazeer. He jumped from the truck and ran in the direction. From a distance, one could observe Nazeer's tiny figure moving up and down, left and right, like a pixel in an old 8-bit game. Soon he was back in the truck. False alarm. The truck started again. A few metres ahead, we reached a fork in the road. Right or left, the driver asked. 'Stay on the left,' Nazeer replied, somehow sure that his son had just made the exact same choices. 'I had screamed at him last night,' Nazeer murmured to himself. Shakil wanted to sit in the front with us, and Nazeer, who still had not come to terms with the theft, had dismissed him angrily. That may have set Shakil off. We were now approaching normal driving speed. If indeed Shakil had snuck out with the aim of disappearing—and one could imagine how frustrated a sixteen-year-old like him would feel—we were about to encounter a great tragedy. Shakil's disappearance could also prematurely end my project. The women cooped up in the back, including Shakil's mother, were silent.

'There he is,' Nazeer said with a start. I couldn't see anything. 'He is . . . he is . . . there,' he said pointing ahead. Slowly, in his black khan dress, the figure of Shakil with a stick in hand emerged a few metres ahead. He was walking on the left side of the road.

The driver requested Nazeer, who was by now gritting his teeth in fury, not to hit his son. One could sense, looking at Nazeer, that the man who only a few hours ago had some of his best sheep stolen was ready to take his son apart. Our truck honked and stopped just beside him. Shakil turned around, and before he could say anything Nazeer pulled him in by his arm. 'Don't hit him,' I couldn't help but say reflexively.

Nazeer tapped him lightly on his head. '*Badmaash, saale,*' he said to Shakil, who was giggling now. 'Next time I'll break all your teeth,' he added in a tone that didn't really sound like a warning. We were now on our way to Shopian.

While Shakil was laughing and offering high-fives to me, Nazeer was coordinating with Majeed over the phone. Majeed told him that there had been an accident. A car had run over one of the goats. The driver wasn't ready to pay, but negotiations weren't over yet.

Through a roundabout way we reached the bank of a river in Shopian. Immediately began the back-breaking process of unloading the truck. Majeed and the others would take some time to reach. Meanwhile the pink salty tea had begun to brew. Several other Bakarwals had also pitched their tents nearby.

To our distant right, we could see the Pir Panjal range looming closer. Small houses dotted the hills. The river, comfortingly shallow and coursing down leisurely, was like a balm to frayed nerves.

We were spread out on boulders like washed clothes, when Riyaz reached with the dead goat on his back. He had wrapped it over several times in rags and bits of jute bags, all of which, along with Riyaz's back, were dripping with blood. The women came over with empty vessels. It hadn't occurred to me until then that the dead goat would be our meal. Though they were surrounded by hundreds of goats and sheep, the Bakarwals couldn't afford to slaughter one from their own herd. But this accident had given everyone here—lactating mothers, hard-working men, children and elderly women with their ribs sticking out—a chance at a rare feast.

'The poor thing was pregnant. Soon it would have given birth to a calf,' Majeed said to me. Fleshy bits were shared equally. There was no way to store the meat. So we had to finish it over the next two meals. Later at the river, most of us had our first baths in several days.

In her travels through Old Serbia, Rebecca West talks about a dinner she had with a group of monks. 'Since it was a Friday this was a fast; and for that reason we were given barley soup, a stew of butter beans, a purée of potatoes with onion sauce, a very greasy stew of sardines and spinach, and a mess of rice cooked with fried potatoes.' That was a meal which she really hated. We, on the other hand, were ecstatic about bits of meat cut of a goat that had died in a road accident.

Dinner was a happy event. For once, everyone was smiling. With chunks of meat on their plates, they cracked jokes about their miseries. It wasn't difficult to see how sick and helpless they were. Most of the time there was barely enough to eat. Jalal's daughter Naziya was stricken with stye. Rabeena's chest was full of phlegm. Her ailment was possibly contagious since she and her brother, Rasheed, couldn't ever stop coughing. She was also nursing a newborn with a head as big as a football. Nazeer always suffered from toothache, and his wife Koka from headaches. Majeed was regularly incapacitated by bouts of high fever. To top it all, despite being sleep-deprived from constantly looking out for thieves, they were nonetheless being robbed. But in these rare moments you could see them all come together and share some happiness. All differences, all rebellion dissolved for the time being.

~

Ram ram naal chalenge [We'll walk at an easy peace],' Nazeer said reassuringly. It was a fresh morning, and we had set off again in the direction of Pir Panjal. A bit of exhaustion had set in among all of us. Even the dogs, who were kicked mercilessly on their snouts by little Naziya when they refused to move, were fatigued.

Nazeer said that the harsher stretch was already behind us. What lay ahead was a piece of cake. We were walking along the river bed, sometimes approaching the edge of the river, sometimes spreading far out, to avoid sharp rocks.

The herd which usually functioned as a giant lawn mower—not finding much grass here—was walking faster than usual. We in turn had to walk faster to catch up with them. Soon it became clear that we weren't going to walk '*Ram ram naal*'. Nazeer hadn't told me that the walk over the mostly dried-up river bed was going to be a 10 kilometre obstacle course, which then would be followed by a walk through an icy cold stream, after which we would have to climb up, on all fours, a straight hill that would bring us to Mughal Road.

Shakil and I came quite close to breaking our bones while crossing the stream, which, when I waded into it bare feet, turned out to be deeper and more forceful than I'd assumed. I was right in the middle of it, trying to get a grip on the slippery rocks, when Liyaqat, frustrated with the herd that was understandably unwilling to enter into the icy waters, started throwing them one by one into the stream. In a mad rush to get to the other side the goats charged in my direction like torpedoes, expediting my—ultimately injury-less—landing.

On Mughal Road, we had different challenges to meet; getting the flock to move on one side of the road was one of them. I took charge of one end and with a borrowed stick kept nudging them into a queue. But often panic caused by the horn of a fast-moving truck or the lack of grass on their side of the road would make sheep and goats break ranks. Moreover, one had to ignore all the abuse that came our way from the drivers of cars, trucks, buses, lorries, pick-up vans, emergency vehicles and even motorcycles. Drivers of larger cars especially made a point of halting their vehicles just before the last goat or shepherd as if either should be thankful for not being run over. All of us, including the herd, were still wringing wet.

Every experience on this trip was a revelation for me, but in the time I had to myself on the road, I wondered what this journey meant for my fellow travellers. They were walking along the same path on which seven generations of Majeed's family had walked. Over those centuries, empires had fallen, two world wars had been fought, nation states had come up, and boundaries had been drawn and redrawn. And so much had happened in Kashmir. So much was still happening in Kashmir. During our stay in Pulwama, helicopters, deployed in encounters with militants, had hovered above us all evening. A year ago, I had been to that very place, and from a field opposite to the one in which we spent the night, reported about one of the many funerals that were held for local militants. Over the past few days, on the radio, we had heard reports about encounters breaking out between security forces and militants, often in areas close to us. The old hermit, in a rare act of expressiveness when we happened to be walking together once, moved his thumb across his throat to show what militants had done to three members of his extended family. 'One of them was as old as you,' he said. Majeed would talk about how Bakarwals got beaten up badly by security forces who thought that the nomads were spying for Pakistan. In spite of this, Majeed and Kaka were leading their caravan up and down these mountains. Why? Maybe these mountain trails were their only inheritance. Something that they knew they could, after a lifetime of hard physical and mental labour, pass on to their children. So they had no choice, really, but to remain rooted to their past.

'If we were to board a couple of large trucks, stuff all animals in them, from here it would take us not more than five hours to reach Poonch in Jammu,' Nazeer said while we were walking on Mughal Road.

The goats that were stolen in Pulwama could have, if the Bakarwals had so desired, been sold for enough money to help these people avoid the next two weeks of misery. It would have helped them avoid the possibility of dying or losing their family members on the trek. But the thought of spending money on a luxury such as a hired truck or two wouldn't even have occurred to them. Not even for the sake of the ailing Rabeena, who was jeopardizing her own life along with that of her newborn baby.

Quietly, we continued walking down this historic road, which had been mentioned in accounts written by travellers hundreds of years ago.

In *Ain I Akbari* (published in 1891 by Asiatic Society of Bengal),[6] the final volume of the three-volume biography of Mughal emperor Akbar, *Akbarnama*, his wazir, Abu Fazl Allami, makes a passing remark about a superstition, of adverse weather conditions being caused by the killing of a horse or an ox on Mughal Road.

Allami makes a note of three routes to Kashmir, one of which passes through Pir Panjal, 'which his majesty [Akbar] has thrice traversed on his way to the rose garden of Kashmir. If on these hills an ox or a horse be killed, storm clouds and winds arise with a fall of snow and rain'.

This road is believed to have assumed its present name because it was frequented by Mughal emperors Akbar and his son and successor, Jahangir, who died on this very road while returning from Kashmir to Delhi.

But it is Col H.S. Jarrett, the translator of the book from its original Persian into English, who provides an interesting footnote to the myth, one that connects it to the death of Jahangir.

The superstition regarding the tempest of wind and snow and rain, appears to be connected with that of the *Yedeh* or rain-stone frequently alluded to by Baber, the history of which is given by D'Herbelot. It is of Tartar origin and the virtues of the stone are celebrated in Yarkand and attested by authorities who have never witnessed them. It is said to be found in the head of a horse or a cow, and if steeped in blood

of an animal with certain ceremonies, a wind arises followed
by snow and rain.

The word 'Pir', he goes on to say, means both a saintly man and
a 'pass' through a mountain range. The word 'Panjal' is applied
to a great mountain range. The two words together, 'Pir Panjal',
have come to mean the pass of the Great Range. He refers to the
account of another traveller, a man called Bernier, who crossed Pir
Panjal during Jahangir's time and noted the presence of a hermit
somewhere in the upper reaches.

> The creed he professed was not known, but his powers were
> said to be miraculous and the elements were under his control,
> rain, hail, storm, and wind rising or creasing at his bidding.
> He demanded alms in a tone of authority, and forbade any
> noise being made lest a tempest should be the consequence, an
> experience which Jahangir incurred to his extreme peril through
> disobedience of this injunction.

We would go on to walk for nearly four hours on this stretch of
Mughal Road, a drill made bearable only by the efforts of little
Naziya.

She was a magician. When I climbed up the Mughal Road,
hungry, drenched in cold water, it was she who came up to me
with the offering of an apple. It was enough to keep me going.

The little thing had stuffed her clothing with them. We were
passing through apple orchards, past some branches laden with the
reddest apples were bowing out of the fence. Little Naziya would
quietly move towards an inviting section of a fence and return
with her wraparound shawl looking substantially bigger.

At the end of four hours, we took a left from Mughal Road and
reached the town of Hirpora. From here, we had to trek up into the
mountain jungles for three hours. We finally reached our spot at
around 4 p.m.

Every member of the caravan seemed to have a fixed routine each time we reached one of our halts. The first thing the men did was look for dry firewood. The women, after unburdening their load, would immediately start unfolding the tents, sometimes with the help of their husbands. They would then prepare their kitchens by lighting firewood. The children looked for food. The horses upturned themselves, like fallen beetles, wriggled their limbs and rubbed their backs on ground. The goats and sheep played cool; they just continued munching grass.

We had finally reached the foot of the Pir Panjal range. Here we would rest for the next several days, and allow the herd, which would find little nutrition ahead, to fatten up.

The meat from the dead goat hadn't finished. We got a small serving that night, and for lunch the subsequent afternoon. Concerns over hygiene, which I'd been able to ignore so far, sprang up on seeing Majeed pull out a goat's head from a gunny bag and gently place it on the fire. It gave out a terrible stench, and had its eyes open and tongue out, as if it was stunned to death while blowing raspberries. I asked Majeed whether the head belonged to a freshly slaughtered goat. No, it didn't. Was this then going to be our dinner? 'Ha ha ha, no. This is for the dogs,' he said.

I had roamed around our tents to get an idea of where we were going to live for the next one week. The Bakarwals always halted somewhere close to a stream, and I came across one at a distance. Our tents were pitched at one side of a concave depression. All around were trees that seemed to grow into each other like the jaws of a huge beast. The sky was the deepest blue I'd ever seen. Being in this cup lent us limited access to direct sunlight, only for about four hours, from 10 a.m. to 2 p.m. Night fell by around 6 p.m. and the sky did not light up again until 7 a.m. the next morning.

~

This was the ladies' day. Since all the men had left—some to Shopian to buy groceries, others to nearby mountains with the flock—our camp turned into an all-women's club on the second day. From Doda (Majeed's wife) in her sixties to Naziya who was not even ten yet, almost all of them were together the whole day, chatting for hours while doing odd jobs and attending to each other's hair.

There's a funny anecdote in *Black Lamb and Grey Falcon* about a distressed young hairdresser. It was narrated by a German couple to Rebecca West and her husband as they're moving in a train towards Zagreb, a few years after Hitler took over Germany.

> To cheer him up, the wife told us funny stories about some consequences of *Hitlerismus*. She described how the hairdresser's assistant who had always waved her hair for her had one morning greeted her with tears, and told her that she was afraid she would never be able to attend to her again, because she was afraid she had failed in the examination which she had to pass for the right to practice her craft. She had said to the girl, 'But I am sure you will pass your examination, for you are so very good at your work.' But the girl had answered, 'Yes, I am good at my work! Shampooing can I do, and water-waving can I do, and marcelling can I do, and oil massage can I do, and hair-dyeing can I do, but keep from mixing up Göring's and Goebbels' birthday, that can I not do.

Nazeer returned that evening with a new phone for himself and a pair of rubber shoes, polished to look like leather, for his elder son, Saji, who handed his worn-out shoes to Rashid,. With a heated piece of metal, Rashid immediately began melting bits of the discarded shoes to fill in the blanks of his own shoes. Nobody at the camp ever discarded their worn-out shoes. They stored those pieces of rubber and with them mended their shoes, little ships of Theseus.

With what looked like an early onset of buyer's remorse, Nazeer handed his phone over to Koka. As if he were no longer interested in this expensive and unnecessary device. As if it were not filling him up with guilt.

Both Nazeer and Koka smiled at each other. He was allowed his indulgence. They fit together like 'a work of art', as West said of a Jewish couple she meets in Sarajevo. Nazeer was a strongly built, tall man, almost resembling Balraj Sahni in the 1961 black and white classic *Kabuliwala*. Koka was shorter, frailer and unbearably kind. She had a beatific, disarming smile that could stop wars. It was certainly enough to subdue the anger of Nazeer, who was most feared in the commune after Majeed. Though when Koka herself got angry, she would send her sons and husband flying for cover.

While travelling in Bosnia, West meets a woman whose voice she finds so sweet she calls her 'the Bulbul'. Her husband, Selim, was 'a very tall man with broad shoulders'.

> I could bring forward as evidence the Bulbul and her mate, the two human beings who more than any others that I have ever met have the right arrangement and comforting significance of a work of art.

She says of the Bulbul:

> Had one been cruel enough to point out to her that one would have been happier with a million pounds, and that she was not in a position to supply it, she would for a moment or two really have suffered, and even when she realised that she had been teased her good sense would not have been able to prevent her from feeling a slight distress.

To the demands of her family, to the whims of anyone around her, Koka was indulgent to the point of self-effacement. But she also had a strong sense of her personal space. After putting her family to sleep, she would often stay by the dying kitchen fire, switch on the radio and listen to a Pahadi folk singer whose songs about solitude and separation were always broadcast at such hours. Sometimes in the dead of night she would also look up at the sky and softly converse with someone. Nobody found it odd. Perhaps in their own tents everyone was privately speaking to the night sky.

~

At night, in a remote mountain jungle, a flock of agitated goats can sound like your worst nightmare. A few nights of listening to their guttural howls in the stillness of the night, and you'll wake up one morning feeling slightly altered inside. The only other phenomenon that came close to replicating its shock was Riyaz's sudden bouts of gibberish.

At least thrice every day, Riyaz would abruptly burst into an alien language in staccato rhythms. He did little variations of it in different circumstances—tersely in his sleep, slightly longer while tending to his herd, and the most elaborate version of this babble was reserved for times when he played with his child. Riyaz was never more happy than when he got time with his little Haider, and the boy was never more happy than when he got to torture his father. Haider would tie his father in knots and beat him with a stick, and Riyaz would respond, while guffawing, with long volleys of his incomprehensible speech. A bit like Manto's famous madman Toba Tek Singh, who only spoke variations of '*Upar de gurgur de aiynks de be-dhyaana de mung de daal aaf de laaltain*'.

The next morning, Nazeer decided to go to Shopian again, and this time he was kind enough to take me along. I had been cooped up in our tent for the last three days and was desperately looking for a chance to stretch my limbs. It took us forty minutes of a downhill walk to reach Hirpora town. We turned right and walked a couple of kilometres towards Shopian. We came close to the house of a person Nazeer said he had to deliver goat's milk to. This person's house was on a hilltop. Nazeer asked me to wait while he made the visit.

After waiting out in the cold for five minutes, I lost patience and decided to look for him.

Walking uphill, I came across a huge flock of goat and sheep, bigger than what Nazeer and his family had. There was only one large tent there and behind it goats were being assembled by handsome and relatively elegant-looking boys. The insides of the tent could have passed off as a temporary shelter for a visiting prince. Expensive-looking utensils were placed in neat rows in what was a clearly defined kitchen area. Inside were placed large, intricately designed carpets, on one side of which I found Nazeer sitting. He got up as he saw me, and bade farewell to an old man who had an air of authority about him. Nazeer shook and kissed his hands and came out. Soon we were back on the road. 'Who was he?' I asked. 'Listen. Don't tell anyone. I mean anyone. The person whom you saw is a very popular *pir*. Just like you are top-class Brahman. He is top-class Bakarwal. He tells the future.' So what did the old man say to Nazeer? 'That I can't tell you. But don't you speak to anyone about this pir or our visit.' Soon we found a ride in a shared taxi up to Shopian.

In about twenty minutes, we came across the same riverbank from where we had to trek eight hours to reach Hirpora. After a few more pick-ups, when the taxi was full, the driver switched on a popular Haryanvi number. I don't know if the driver or my fellow occupants understood the suggestive lyrics of the song but nobody seemed to find it out of place. After crossing the snaky bends of the mountains with some caution, the driver was going at breakneck speed on the plains. All the eight fellow passengers went 'Bismil-lah' at the first speed-breaker, when we were thrown up in the air like rice in a winnowing fan. Two burqa-clad ladies at the back chastised the driver quite loudly in Urdu, '*Itni lambi daadi hai iski fir bhi . . . Bismil-lah . . . kitni zor se chalata hai* [He has such a long beard . . . Bismil-lah . . . still, look at how fast he drives].' The lady next to her responded, '*Ye log bohot lalchi hote hain. Insaan ko kabhi laalach nahi karna . . . Bismil-lah* [These are very greedy people. A man should never be greedy . . . Bismil-lah].' But the words didn't seem to have any effect on him. He went over several more speed-breakers and the fellow passengers repeated their chorus with increasing passion. It took us forty-five minutes to reach the Shopian bus stand.

While Nazeer looked for a small jacket for Rashid, I took a walk around the main square which was shadowed by a huge mosque on one side. It was crowded with locals and some other Bakarwals trying to bargain with street vendors selling fruits, vegetables, clothes, and hovering curiously around that crown jewel of Indian bazaars: a cart with a random assortment of lighters, knives, combs, nail-cutters and other such mundane items.

We ran many minor errands for the next hour or so, some of them quite unnecessary. Nazeer scolded me for almost buying salt without bargaining. We went around looking for cheap salt in the entire town. It was a matter of no more than Rs 15 or 20 but he wouldn't relent. Finally we returned to the original vendor who let us have the salt at a discount of Rs 10. Nazeer was proud of himself. We then went to a phone shop where he bought a memory card loaded with songs, movie clips and entire TV shows in low resolution. Rashid and I sat that night and watched decades-old episodes of *Alif Laila* on Nazeer's phone. It turned out to have greater novelty for me, who had last seen these episodes as a child, than for Rashid, who had quite recently seen them on some other phone.

Having finished our chores, we went to a tea shop and treated ourselves to bread and tea. It seemed like ages since I'd sat on a chair. We felt like royalty. Nazeer, in fact, hung up on his cousin while sipping his fourth cup of tea. 'I'm busy in a meeting. Don't you understand?' he said to him.

After several rounds of tea, we prepared for the return journey. It was evening and there was a mad rush for the last few shared taxis. Somehow, both of us made it inside one. I looked up and caught a glimpse of my decrepit self in the rear-view mirror. The other passengers stared at me as I chuckled to myself. It was late into the night when we reached our camp.

That night we sat over our tea well after dinner. Majeed, Riyaz, both the Altafs, Nazeer and his two sons.

'So tell me, how did you get here from Delhi?' Majeed asked.

'In an aeroplane,' I said.

The conversation continued as I responded to questions that were to do with the size of an aeroplane, the number of people who could sit in it, the price of the ticket, and so on. I gave them arbitrary figures. They started calculating.

'It's a really rewarding business isn't it, flying aeroplanes? The pilot must be making more in one trip than a bus driver makes in his life,' Nazeer said. 'He's making lakhs of rupees for a three-hour job.'

They were also curious about Delhi. What did it look like? How did it look from an aeroplane? Were there mosques in Delhi? Were there streams? Did Muslims live in Delhi? But their curiosity was heightened when someone mentioned Prime Minister Narendra Modi's name.

'How big is his house?'

'Very big. It's bigger than any house you have ever seen.'

'Why does he live in such a big house?'

'Because he's the prime minister. He's entitled to a very large house.'

'Could we go meet him?'

'I don't know really. He's quite busy. But you can try. Who knows?'

After our tea, we broke off for the night. Rashid slept after watching three or four episodes of *Alif Laila*. I wasn't quite feeling sleepy so I just lay there watching the night sky. Everyone had dozed off. About half an hour later I heard a rustle. A match was struck. I turned around to look. Behind me, Nazeer was taking a deep puff of a bidi. I smiled to myself.

~

'Aar Aye Ess Etch Eye Dee.' Rashid was making some sketches on a piece of paper when I offered to teach him the English spelling of his name. I wrote it down, asked him to look at the letters and memorize them. 'Aar Ae Ess Etch Eye Dee . . . Rashid,' he repeated after me. Although I taught him the alphabet, I strongly suspected that he couldn't tell the letters apart and had only memorized the sounds.

Slowly, others appeared around us. Saji, the Altafs, Shakil, Majeed's youngest son, Zakir. All of them wanted to learn to write their names. I gave them bits of paper with their names written on them. Rashid, the original pupil, wanted to outdo everyone else. He started writing the letters with mad fury. On the ground with a stick, on Shakil's face, secretly in my notebook, inside the pages of *Black Lamb and Grey Falcon*, till I had to intervene. A page inside the book still bears his handwriting, 'R A S H I' with the missing 'D'. But Rashid wouldn't stop. He resumed writing his name on his left hand and soon his arm was covered with letters. Shakil wrote his name on his kurta but that's where he stopped.

Rashid's father had given him a broken-down mobile phone a few days ago. I observed from the corner of my eye as Rashid opened up his phone, cut the slip of paper on which I'd written his name to just the right size, and tucked it behind the battery, while mumbling, 'Aar Aye Ess Etch Eye Dee . . . Rashid.'

He was particularly chirpy that day since he'd learnt to spell his name in English. 'Eat as much as you want now that you're living with us. Don't hesitate to ask for anything. Ask for whatever you want, anytime,' Rashid declared over lunch.

Later in the evening, when we were having tea and bread, Rashid couldn't stop chirping, '*Ye dekh roti. Roti pe lag raha hai grease hai. Grease jaaanta hai? . . . Tum log chai mein duud daalta hai? . . . Tum ye noon chai ghar pe banata hai? Hum kehwa bhi banata hai, Lifton bhi* [Look at this bread. Looks like it has been greased. Do you know what grease is? Do you guys add milk to your tea? Do you make this pink salty tea back home? We make both types, kehwa and Lipton].' From somewhere Rashid got his hands on an old Hot Wheels toy car, which everyone else identified as a tempo. He spent the rest of his time playing with it.

We were to resume our journey that day, but Nazeer got a call from a relative who was camping ahead. He told Nazeer that a wild beast had devoured two of his goats. The men decided to wait another day.

I didn't know till Koka came over to ask me whether I'd got any vegetables from my excursion to Shopian that we were running out of food. She must have tortured herself over this for hours. It was a Friday and Riyaz was going to Hirpora's masjid to offer prayers. I went along with him and returned in the evening with a sack-load of vegetables. Koka was delighted. I asked her whether I should have brought vegetables for the others. It wasn't necessary, she said, but given that everyone had seen me with vegetables, she went around distributing some potatoes and tomatoes.

Since the Bakarwals were living in a commune and depended on each other, nobody could be seen eating more vegetables than the other, applying greater amounts of ghee on their chapattis than the others. The curries everywhere were uniformly thin. Which is why perhaps, despite handing over at least a week's supply of vegetables, oils and spices, we still had barely enough to eat. Every family maintained a secret stash of walnuts and apples. Nobody would eat a fruit in front of others. One day, Koka, thin as she was, tried to supplement her family's income by walking all the way down to Hirpora to peel walnut fruits for a pittance. She seemed happy that night but because of the exertion she kept panting even in her sleep. The dye from the fruit blackened her hands for a long time.

The next day, the men again thought of moving ahead but the relative told them that it had started snowing in the peaks. Again we delayed the departure, though everyone seemed happy that they had avoided being caught in a snowstorm on the peaks.

'Don't you feel homesick?' I asked Shaheen, Majeed's daughter, once, feeling a little homesick myself. 'No, why?' she asked. 'Because we have been stuck here ever since we arrived. Wouldn't it be good if we all reached home, ate to our heart's content and slept throughout the day?'

Shaheen said that life back home, at their temporary summer residence, was even worse. They would have to carry out repair work on their houses, which they hadn't seen in the last six months. They would have to tend to their fields because the maize crop would be ready for harvest by the time they returned. And a stationary flock of hundreds of sheep and goats was a bigger pain than a flock on the move.

I got on well with her. She must have been Rabeena's age, around nineteen or so. But unlike Rabeena, she was always bursting with energy. She had a sense of humour and a strong sense of self. She was angry with me when I paid for her groceries once. Shaheen also had a strong sense of belonging for which I envied her greatly. It wasn't just a meek acceptance of fate. She had figured out what her destiny was, where she had come from and who her people were, and she defended all these things quite fiercely.

I once asked her if she knew what her name meant. She didn't. I told her and in order to impress her, began reciting Iqbal's '*Tu Shaheen hai, parvaaz hai kaam tera . . .*' But she walked off before I could finish the couplet.

It rained for the next three days. Rains meant that our tents were flattened to keep the water away. The smoke from the firewood choked all the occupants inside, but nobody could go out and risk getting drenched, except to get essentials like firewood or to answer nature's call. Temperatures were plummeting and no one could walk around without blankets.

Riyaz had bought, after two days of scouting in the Shopian market, the cheapest pheran, a woollen gown, or what the Bakarwals called a '*juba*', for his son, Haider. Going forward, when we began our ascent, the temperature was only going to drop further. But Riyaz could not afford more than Rs 250 for a juba to protect his son from the cold. Little Haider now roamed around in a tiny juba and a small woollen cap.

Most others who could not afford a cap wore headbands made out of strips of cloth. Our camp looked like a Rambo fan club. Illnesses were also taking hold. Koka couldn't get up because of her severe headaches. She kept repeating Saji's name so dispiritingly for days that I felt like violently shaking her out of her delirium. Majeed and Doda got terribly high fevers. Nazeer's toothache returned. The hermit couldn't stop coughing and handed over his bundle of bidis to me. But the most severely stricken of them all was Rabeena.

She was strikingly beautiful. Rabeena clearly hated having only one set of worn-out clothes, but you wouldn't have noticed the hanging threads or the stitches on her dress easily, with such pride did she carry herself.

But hers was a tragic story. She lived with an alpha male who, within just a couple of years of their marriage, had lost interest in her. She also did not have any money to treat their child, whose ever-growing head looked on the verge of bursting. She cooked, washed, folded and unfolded the tent, packed and unpacked all her household items, and carried her few-months-old child over dangerous mountains, by herself. All along, you could hear her strained, grainy breathing. She coughed incessantly. And she laughed sometimes with such ferociousness that it seemed like the onset of a nervous breakdown.

The day when all the ladies went to the stream to bathe, when they combed each other's hair, gossiped and just lay around, Rabeena was the only woman who didn't come out of her tent. She was also the only person in the entire camp who did not hide her disgust with her life.

George Orwell, in *The Road to Wigan Pier*,[7] describes such a woman whose fleeting glimpse he catches from his train as it passes by a poor suburb. He sees her trying to clear a blocked drain pipe with a stick. He sees in her 'the most desolate, hopeless expression'. This leads him on to believe 'that we are mistaken when we say that "It isn't the same for them as it would be for us," and that people bred in the slums can imagine nothing but the slums. For what I saw in her face was not the ignorant suffering of an animal. She knew well enough what was happening to her—understood as well as I did how dreadful a destiny it was to be kneeling there in the bitter cold on the slimy stones of a slum backyard, poking a stick up a foul drain-pipe.'

We spent nine days in those jungles before Manzoor, a young friend of Nazeer's, arrived at the camp. He had made the reverse journey from Jammu. He told us that the way ahead was clear now. I was in awe of his courage and energy. I wondered how he'd walked across Pir Panjal alone, in a day, and was back on his feet to return the next day. I gazed after him for a long time as he bade farewell to everyone and in great lunges sped up a nearby hill.

While others accepted the statement in a matter-of-fact way, I was quite ecstatic. The spirit of adventure was beckoning us out there. As was the spirit of hygiene.

All of us had been living in this bowl-ish landscape for the past ten days. Personal space was shrinking fast. It was perhaps only a matter of time before we began running into each other while answering nature's calls.

I laughed to myself as I thought of how V.S. Naipaul would have suffered and described this place were he to live here for as long. He would have filled up pages with 'Excrement!' 'Shit!' 'Excrement!'

The greatest writer of our time couldn't look past a pile of turd and sometimes he talked about it with a crazed, wide-eyed hysteria. If the readers of Naipaul ever laughed their guts out, it was in passages such as this from *India: A Wounded Civilisation*.[8]

> Through these sections we walked without speaking, picking our way between squirts and butts and twists of human excrement . . .

It was the business of the sweepers to remove excrement, and until the sweepers came, people were content to live in the midst of their own excrement . . . Two starved Bombay street cows had been tethered there, churning up human excrement with their own; and now, out of this bog, they were being pulled away by two starved women, to neighbourhood shouts, the encouraging shouts of a crowd gathering around this scene of isolated, feeble frenzy, theatre in the round on an excremental stage.

~

On the eleventh day, we started the ascent at 9 a.m., in the same direction that Manzoor had gone the previous day. We were walking through dense jungles spread over some sharp-edged hills. The echoes of birds, which made sounds like old creaking fans, rang throughout the jungle. We walked over large tree trunks that must have fallen on the ground with great force. After a while, I began calculating, out of exhaustion, which would consume less energy—climbing over the tree trunks or walking around them. It was an hour before the vegetation started to thin. Nazeer, who was leading the horses, was most likely still busy back at the camp packing up stuff and loading it on the horses.

Then we came upon what was an almost vertical green wall. As I began climbing it, some muscles, which I had never felt before, began to issue SOS signals. The calves hurt the most. I was sure I couldn't walk beyond the cusp, and thankfully, Shakil and Liyaqat decided to take a break there. It was the top of a small-sized mountain which overlooked, on the other side, the biggest meadow I'd ever seen. It was like looking at Srinagar from the mountain where we first camped, except the entire city was replaced with a thick green carpet. For as far as you could see, the carpet undulated into small folds but never showed a tear. Sprinkled on it, far below, were many white-coloured tents. You could hear echoes of dogs barking and men shouting to each other.

Sheep and horses were munching grass. It was such a picturesque view that you could swear you'd seen it somewhere before. Perhaps on a badly distempered office wall.

From here we began walking on a wide path overlooking those tents. We came across several more tents and some very basic structures built of rock where many other Bakarwals had broken their journey. We were walking over a dried-up river bed deep into a valley from which you could hear faint noises coming from shifting dots of people. We had left dense vegetation and tall trees far behind, and now the grass was also thinning out. Our breathing also became slightly strained. All signs that we were ascending.

It was around 1 p.m. when we ran into a heavy storm. It had probably snowed up in the mountains again. The temperature was dropping quite fast and the sun was disappearing. Having left the grassy meadows behind, we were now walking on a narrow, dusty path surrounded only by large boulders.

The tops of the mountains on either side of us were covered with a strange red-coloured grass that looked like lava. From the river bed we could now hear the sound of a raging stream. It was tough finding one's feet on the narrow path in the dark, with the sun in freefall. The path had begun to shrink even more. Two people couldn't walk side by side. We were wriggling in a worm-like formation.

A few metres ahead, as I looked up, I saw sheep in front of me jump. One after another, like a wave. One of the Altafs, whom I hadn't noticed perched on a small rock above, shouted at me, '*Kuud* [jump]!' The flock behind me didn't give me time to halt and comprehend why exactly he was asking me to jump. '*Kuud!*' he shouted again. Suddenly, I noticed the ground under my feet coming to an abrupt end. Solid ground resumed after a gap of a couple of feet. I jumped to the other side, and in a split second noticed two things. First, there was blood on the landing. Someone among us was clearly injured. Second, what I had just jumped over was a straight drop hundreds of feet down to the rocks. There was a third realization that came subsequently. Hundreds of impatient hooves were about to jump towards me. I had to immediately press forward. What happened instead was that I froze, looked at Altaf and meekly said, '*Khuun* [blood].' For some reason my body wouldn't take another step. Altaf ran towards me, offered his hand and pulled me to safety. '*Khuun*,' I said again with a face that I imagine was white with fear.

'We are all fine. This is from a goat. I don't think it will be able to make it,' Altaf said. The colour was returning on my face. A few seconds later, I was even quietly celebrating. What could be better than some meat for dinner! The temperature would plummet in the night. Not a bad time for another feast.

It was around 3 p.m. We were to travel till 6 p.m. that evening, but Majeed ordered everyone to stop and pitch their tents. The risks of continuing forward were quite high, he said. 'We don't want to be caught in a storm in higher areas.' We were sheltered on one side by a giant boulder which must have been at least 8 metres high, and of roughly the same breadth. Somebody had taken refuge under it not too long ago. Quite close to where we were standing there were the remains of a fireplace—burnt wood, and the claws of some animal. A cold wind was still blowing with great force, though a bit of sun had come out now. It was almost impossible to pitch tents against the force of the wind. But somehow, every family was able to do it. They had to. They didn't have a choice.

I was looking at the raging, frothing stream from the edge of what was a rather tall cliff when I spotted Liyaqat and Nazeer down below. They were struggling to get to the other side of the mighty stream and I couldn't figure out why. Just when I was wondering when and how they had climbed down so quickly, I saw Naseem and Rabeena at the bank of the stream with their huge water pots. In a few moments, even Koka appeared with her pot. She would have weighed far less than the pot of water she was about to carry all the way up.

Shaheen and Rashid were trying to light fires near each tent. They had covered themselves with at least two blankets each. As had Saji and Ashraf, who were tending to the flock far above us on a nearby mountain. The women balancing pots of water over their heads appeared one by one several minutes later. In shame I moved out of their sight. On the other side of the boulder, horses were still falling to the ground, upturning and moving their limbs in the air. I saw Liyaqat and Nazeer climb up the other mountain and approach what seemed like a small hut. It was after a long time that they returned with arms full of firewood. Since there were no trees around, some Bakarwal who had no use for the firewood he had carried, had neatly bundled it and kept it under the hard roof for fellow Bakarwals, away from sun and rain.

We finished dinner quickly. Koka was unwell so everyone had only a few morsels. Rashid ate half the rice on his plate and curled up in his bed. I was very tired, but quite hungry still. I considered his unfinished plate of rice for some time, looked around and then ate it with relish.

'*Ye le, Lifton chai garam karti hai* [Take this, the milky tea warms you up],' Nisaar said, handing me a cup of tea which he had brought from his tent. Three cups later, I felt alive again. The stream below sounded liked a jet taking off. There was no sleep to be had. It was really cold, with icy winds still blowing forcefully. Liyaqat and one of the Altafs were up all night, talking beside the fire outside our tent. Nazeer too chatted with them. Rashid kept coughing. From a distance one could hear Rabeena coughing violently as well. One could only hope to remain warm coiled up inside blankets in a foetal position till it was time to leave.

Soon it was. I may not have slept for more than an hour when Nazeer shook me awake and handed me a cup of tea. It was time to go. My bottom felt numb, probably from contact with the large stone on which I'd slept. From a distance I heard faint whistles. It was Majeed! I quickly put on shoes and rolled up my sleeping bag, but Nazeer stopped me.

'It's too dark. Majeed left fifteen minutes ago. He is not as near as you think,' Nazeer said. So I was stuck with the cavalry then. We began packing everyone else's stuff and loading it on the horses. It took another half an hour or so before Liyaqat realized that three of his horses had gone missing. Horses were priceless, especially at this altitude. Liyaqat left with the hermit in the dark to find them. It was well after sunrise and we were ready to move, when someone spotted Liyaqat on top of a mountain trying to direct his horses down. '*Wo raha* [There],' Ashraf said as all of us stood looking up at Liyaqat as if he was Superman.

He was drenched in sweat when he came down. Without a pause, the caravan started to move. I asked Nazeer how long the day's journey would be. 'Ooooo,' he said. '*Abhi to baat hi mat karo* [Don't even get me started].'

The stream had disappeared again and we were walking on the dry river bed, on the floor of which you could see round stones of all sizes and colours—black, green, grey, pink, red, blue and white. Doda was racing ahead. She moved as if climbing on the boulders, stepping down and climbing again was the most natural thing to do for a sixty-year-old. Having come down to the river bed, we lost the sun. Even the walk wasn't bringing any warmth to the bones. It was a really desolate, silent valley that we were walking through, where the only noises were made by the stones crunching under our feet and by Rabeena's coughing.

Fatigue was setting in quickly, so I made a plan. The horses were walking in three groups with the one led by Nazeer marching in front. I would walk quickly, catch up with Nazeer's group and keep pace with it for as long as I could. When I began to tire, I'd catch some breath and start walking with the second group. Then try and get back with Nazeer again. The third I'd kept for reserve.

The constantly chattering teeth and numbness in the body was sickening. Four hours would pass before the sun rose above the shoulders of the mountains to our left. We passed several streams, climbed over many hills, and walked a kilometre through a thick outgrowth of ankle-high spiny-leafed bushes which left deep scratches on the ankles. Doda was out of sight now and I was walking with the third batch of horses. 'Don't get left behind. No one will be able to find you here,' Liyaqat warned as he walked by with his horses.

Shortly after noon, we reached a really big rock, beside which flowed very slowly a river of solid ice. It was an immense climb. At almost every turn on that rock, I felt tremors of what felt like an oncoming heart attack. Naseem, the Altafs, Rashid, Naziya and the two dogs passed me by one by one. The only driving force was the dread of losing sight of them and freezing to death in this empty valley. It took forever but I climbed all the way up and collapsed on the stony floor. I was prostrate on the ground and, except for the rapid heaving of my chest, absolutely still. I needed water. I reached for the half-empty bottle tied to my backpack. Rashid looked at me expectantly. It didn't take me more than a couple of seconds to empty the bottle while he stared at me in disbelief.

Koka had woken up early to make rotis. She handed me one. It was full of red chillies. I couldn't have asked for anything else. I had another and wouldn't have minded more except there were many more mouths to be fed. After a break of half an hour, we were up on our feet again. A few metres ahead of us was a straight wall of loose black gravel, covered with patches of snow, which we now had to climb. I pleaded with Liyaqat to carry my backpack, but he in turn handed me his own bag since he had to carry the injured goat. The damn thing hadn't died yet. There I was then, down on all fours, climbing the wall with two bags on my back.

I had asked Majeed the previous day whether there had been any major accidents on this route. 'Yes, two decades ago some twenty-five Bakarwals had been swept away by strong winds somewhere around here. Their bodies were never found.'

Black gravel was turning into sludge because of the melting snow. Instead of climbing, I realized after some time that I was slowly descending. As I looked upward I found Naziya and Naseem standing at the top laughing at me. I reached out sideways for the drier patches. My entire body—the face, hands, legs—rang like a gong, so violently was my heart trying to break free from its cage. Almost everyone was out of sight now. With one final burst of energy I managed to roll over to the top. I was still wobbly when I stood up and saw in front of me yet another climb, a strangely shaped large rock that must have been some 10 metres high, through the voids of which everyone was climbing further up. Liyaqat and the goat with the broken leg were also trying to catch their breath. The fairly large goat was looking more worn out than him. He asked me to go ahead first. I did and in a minute I was there. This was the top. The summit.

What a view it had! The space on which I sat was smaller than a barstool. It was quite like the space that I as a child had imagined would be the top of the world. Behind me was a panoramic view of the desolate valley we had just left behind. Ahead of us was an expanse of several shades of green. The summit marked the boundary between Jammu and Kashmir. Slowly, some other colours, apart from shades of green, revealed themselves. Hues of blue, grey and brown. The view of the forest below was blocked near the horizon by thick, dark clouds. The rocks around me were covered with a dark red grass. It is this grass that must have made the mountains, which we had passed on the way here, look like fountains of lava. Blades of this grass had the deepest hue of red and were very brittle, like the petals of dried rose.

'Sometimes a country will for days keep its secrets from a traveller,' West writes in her travelogue, 'showing him nothing but its surfaces, its grass, its trees, the outside of its houses. Then suddenly it will throw him a key and tell him to go where he likes and see what he can.'[9]

The path ahead ran along a mountain, and it was so narrow that I had to tilt towards the slope while walking so that I'd fall to safety even if I tripped. I hadn't walked 10 metres before I felt the urge to kick a small stone, a childish urge to see it roll down the mountain. The stone stayed put, I tumbled. *'Ladka rud gayo*

[The boy's tripped],' the hermit's wife, Sharifa Begum, shouted as she walked past. I got up immediately, more embarrassed than hurt, and took a moment to soak in my surroundings. I saw that the mountains all around, from the higher reaches where I stood, till as far down as was visible, were lined with many such parallel narrow pathways, so they looked like interconnected pyramids.

I started in Sharifa's direction but soon lost sight of her. The parallel pathways were like a maze. Some of them ended abruptly, which meant I had to climb up or down to take a relatively safer route forward. Sometimes there was no option but to jump, from one tightrope to another. Often Sharifa Begum or Liyaqat would spot me from far away and shout instructions—'Move up, up, there, get on that'—to get me to a safer route.

The descent wasn't as easy as I had hoped. A totally different set of muscles had begun to issue stress signals. Due to the nature of the descent, my body weight was crushing my toes against the roof of my shoes. To avoid this, I started walking sideways, but one couldn't get far quickly that way. Over an hour later, the mountains gave way to a hill, the top of which was covered with loose stones, as if some great force had smashed large stones to pieces over this hill. Walking over it was even more cumbersome since the ground under the feet kept slipping. I had decided to rest a little way down for some time when I noticed small chips of stones falling around me. Very quickly, larger stones were rolling down the hill with great momentum. I looked up. It was the goats. They had begun to amble around the hilltop and were now sending stones shooting down like missiles. I had to make a dash for it. Running straight down was out of the question because the ground was quite shaky and I was almost certain to trip and fall face first, and keep falling all the way down. So I had to start sliding downwards wherever the terrain permitted.

I had now reached a lower hill on the far end of which I saw Liyaqat resting. We sat together for a few minutes. Black clouds had begun to gather on our far right and soon they began thundering with deafening booms. What luck! 'Majeed has asked for the tents to be pitched at the bottom of this hill but we won't be able to make it in time,' he said. I placed a bet with him, more out of hope than anything else, that we'd make it there before tents were up. The clouds were pacing ahead, as were we. It was around 3 p.m. when we joined the rest of the caravan. Beside little stone houses, Nazeer, Majeed, the hermit and Rabeena were putting up their tents. Soon, we were inside Nazeer's tent, having tea, shortly before it began to snow. The tall hill that I had just struggled down was behind us. Ahead lay an immense sloping valley, to our right were smaller hills that we had to go over the following morning, and a gentle stream flowed to our left. This time I helped Naseem and Rabeena fetch water. This was the valley of Gurbattan, Majeed said.

Night fell quickly and, since we were in the beginning of a new lunar phase, we were in pitch darkness. There were a dozen of us huddled inside Nazeer's tent because it was so cold and there was so much to talk about. When it was time to retire after dinner I walked out of the tent, my knees feeling creaky, not to speak of the bruises on both my legs. There was in the sky the entire Milky Way in all its splendour. I needed someone to share the moment with. 'Listen,' I said to Altaf with great affection, 'do you see the stars above? They're called *stars* in English. You know how far they are? You can't imagine. They're very, very far. And you know what? Some of these stars, which are twinkling so brightly, may not even exist actually.' Altaf heard me and got up. I couldn't be happier. I had obviously piqued his interest just enough for us to sit out and have a conversation. We would exchange names of constellations in English and Gojri. Altaf came out of the tent, looked at me, and squatted. He had come out to pee.

The injured goat was holding on to its life. But another smaller goat had taken ill. Majeed had deposited its almost lifeless body with Nazeer, who was now taking care of it as if it were his own child. He gave it warm milk, injected it with medicine and covered it with blankets. Every few seconds he would stroke its back, trying to bring it to life. It was probably dying of a poisonous insect bite, Nazeer said.

Well after dinner when everyone had left, Koka started talking to Nazeer in whispers. She seemed concerned about something. Once in a while they would turn towards me. I could sense that something was wrong and it had to do with me. Altaf and Nisaar came to pick me after some time. Nazeer had told me about the shortage of space for the night. Our stay here was brief and members of many families who hadn't unfolded their tents wished to spend the night in his tent. Altaf, Nisaar and I had to share space inside one of the stone huts.

The hut repelled us with its stench. It stank like a slaughterhouse and was probably used as one. The absence of windows, one could tell, had preserved the smell. We brushed goat poop off the floor and covered ourselves with blankets. I couldn't sleep. I kept looking at the doorless entrance in dread of goats who I feared would assemble in the hut in great numbers, to escape the intense cold outside and then . . . start chewing my blanket? The old hermit was on guard all night. In between brief spells of sleep I heard the hermit coughing and his footsteps approaching and moving away. Sometimes at the entrance I saw a tiny dancing dot of light which I imagined was his bidi.

~

Majeed's screams woke everyone up the next morning. 'Didn't I tell you to keep watch? Couldn't you have been up one night? Why didn't you wake me up if you were feeling so sleepy?' I caught Nazeer running up and down and asked him for some details. 'I told you about this beast who roams in this area. He devoured two of our goats,' he said. There were many versions of what this beast looked like. Kaka, who had been up all night for precisely this, thought it looked like a bear. Nazeer's descriptions fit that of a leopard. At the crime scene, a few metres away from our stone hut, all one could make out was bits of legs and chewed-up reddish bones, which the guard dogs were attending to with great relish. There was more bad news. The goat in Nazeer's care hadn't survived. But a sheep had given birth early in the morning. The tiny lamb, still reeling after its delivery, was tucked in a small bag on Majeed's shoulders. It was around 5 a.m. In an hour we were marching towards the hills on our right.

It was an ocean of hills. We kept climbing up and down till, at the break of dawn, we could no longer see the beautiful valley of Gurbattan behind us. There was still no trace of any vegetation around. The herd—and I had come to really admire their tenacity by now, as they had swept over landmass like no other species except maybe the bisons of America—was growing impatient for food. Hills gave way to a sea of boulders. For as far as you could see, there was nothing else. These boulders were so huge, and so many, that you couldn't see or guess how far above the ground you were moving. Or rather, tap dancing, as Majeed was doing while moving from one boulder to another, quite unlike the gracelessness with which Shakil and I were jumping and fastening ourselves to boulders like geckos. While tap dancing, with the lamb on his shoulders, Majeed was also farting like a trombone. It was a performance like no other.

I fell down several times while witnessing it. My legs often slipped off the smooth curves of the boulders and got stuck at odd angles. 'It's those cheap shoes of yours,' Majeed said, trying to comfort me. On some of the boulders you could see yellow paint marks, made perhaps by Bakarwals for the benefit of their fellow nomads. But they weren't wholly accurate as I found out when, after some rest, I followed the signs to get back with the rest of the caravan, and was instead led to the edge of a cliff.

After around two hours of walking on the boulders, we reached a meadow. Here we took a short break as the famished goats and sheep got busy munching grass. The newly born lamb was doing well too. It had begun making its first noises while trying to wriggle out of the cloth in which Majeed had wrapped it. He undid the cloth and let the thing totter around for a while.

As I lay prostrate on the ground, my mind went back to the unearthly image of Koka that I had seen earlier that morning. Her nose was wrapped with layers of dark polythene. It looked like she had grown a beak overnight. Nazeer explained that due to the storm there was a chance of lightning striking around them and her metal nose pins could attract a fatal bolt. '*Jungle mein bohot setting ke saath rehna padta hai* [One has to live in the jungles with a lot of care],' Nazeer told me. He liked saying this to me every now and then.

Once, he offered the advice of not taking a leak standing up. Did it sound embarrassing? Not until Koka too joined in. 'What he's saying is correct. Do it sitting down.' They had seen a lot of violence in their lives, they said. In the off chance that militants hiding in the jungles saw us, their attention, Nazeer and Koka argued, would straightaway go to the man urinating in a manner unlike most Muslims. That wouldn't be good for me or for them. '*Jungle mein bohot setting ke saath rehna padta hai.*'

The concern about my identity was shared by many in the caravan. Some, like Altaf, proposed giving me a new name for the duration of our journey. 'I'll call you Sanjay,' Altaf said, not really getting the point. He said he had named me after his childhood friend whom he had not seen in years. Rashid came up with his proposal—'*Muh Saaf* [Clean Mouth]'—because I brushed twice a day. Once in a while, he would prefix this with 'Oye' and as far as he was concerned that was my name.

'But what will we say he's doing with us?' Ashraf asked. It was a good point. 'We'll say he's one of those roving government school teachers,' Majeed said. So there, I was given two names and a profession.

My legs couldn't carry me any more but we had to start moving again. The flock had trimmed the grass with a fine-toothed comb. The little lamb was back in the bag. Majeed led us with his stately gait over another set of boulders. We then climbed a huge hill, followed by a higher one, and then one higher still. Weren't we, after scaling Pir Panjal, supposed to be descending, I asked Majeed? It'll be easier from here on, he said. The roof of the third hill was covered with ice, which was melting at certain points. Gradually hundreds of footsteps changed it to slush. I felt the weight of my boots, picking up mud, increase to a point where I was playing tug-of-war with gravity.

An hour later, Majeed, Shakil and I were looking down a mountain with loose stones, springs, waterfalls, abrupt edges, and no apparent route to surmount all these obstacles. 'You wanted descent,' Majeed said, 'here it is.' He said he had to take a longer route with the herd. I looked down hard. Shakil burst out laughing. With his trembling stick and unsteady frame he pushed forth. 'We brothers will have a lot of fun,' he said. I turned to Majeed and begged him to take me along. 'No, you go with Shakil, he knows the way.'

'I won't be a bother at all,' I begged. No, he said.

'Let's go,' Shakil said.

He couldn't stop laughing. We fell several times. I wished he had fallen more often. The bottom of the mountain seemed to recede further with each step. Half an hour later we were still descending and the base of the mountain was still running away. But at least now I could see a stream below, which was a good sign because, as I had learnt almost instinctively, it would be somewhere along this stream that we would eventually pitch our tents. On the far end of the stream I saw Liyaqat with the injured white goat and Riyaz following him. That goat seemed to have more love for life than all of us put together.

It took forever, but eventually we were progressing on a more or less level path. Nazeer and others with the horses had made rapid progress down the mountain and were now with us. We were walking along the stream. On the other side there were huts, the temporary shelters for Bakarwals, with beautifully designed colourful motifs.

Half a kilometre ahead, Nazeer decided to pitch tents. Barely had we rested when it started to rain. In a few seconds, without a roof over our heads, we were caught in a hailstorm. The only person to have set up her tent was Naseem. No fewer than twenty of us quickly crawled into it. Poor Naseem ran out of food very soon. Rashid came looking for lunch but there wasn't any.

Just above us on the slope was a small shrine of an old Bakarwal fakir. 'We call it a *baithak*. It was an old Bakarwal, Bhai Mohammad Shafi. He used to walk on this very route until one day he decided to stop here for good and meditate. Around twenty years ago he died on this spot. We pray to him for safe passage,' Nazeer said.

The rains subsided, and though it was still overcast, we could see far into the distance. The mountains ahead weren't as imposing as those we had left behind. Majeed said we were somewhere near Buddal. We had crossed from Hirpora into Chor Gali, Kule, Burj, Shukhni Pahad, Purana Burj, Tikini, Gurbattan, Kogada, Andrachi, Khudre, Kalad, and were now very close to Buddal, he said.

Rashid switched on the radio. A station was playing an old Jagjit Singh ghazal. In about five seconds he twisted the tuner impatiently. I so wanted him to turn it back, but was too tired to argue with him. It was around 5 p.m., so Nazeer called out to Rashid to hand over his 'Radco'. That's what they called a radio. A solar torch light was called 'Baintry'. It was time for Nazeer to tune into a programme called 'Hello Pahadi Farmayish'. Every evening Bakarwals would call up the radio jockey with their problems and request a song. Some would talk mournfully about losing their goats to thieves, some would complain about the illiteracy and backwardness in their community. Some just called to hear themselves on the radio. You could tell by the sonic disturbance.

Over tea at Nazeer's tent, Liyaqat, the Altafs, Jalal, Riyaz and Nisar came over. The conversation moved around to my stay. 'I did not expect you to come so far,' Liyaqat said. I accepted it as a compliment. He recounted the good times, the funny times, and out of the blue, issued me a bit of life advice—don't get too friendly with the Shias. 'I never go to deal with a Shia by myself. They like hanging us [Sunnis] upside down, torturing us and drinking our blood,' Liyaqat said with a straight face. I laughed, alone. 'No, don't think this is a joke. They really practise such witchcraft. They group together and drink a Sunni's blood from a cup,' Liyaqat said. Nazeer not just nodded gravely, he also shared some wisdom about Shia love for black magic. Nobody except me had a smile on their faces. Dinner ended up being a quiet affair.

Later that night, Nazeer told me that the caravan would stay in Buddal for a week. So there was no point in me wasting my time here. 'You have already seen all there is to see,' he said.

'You're asking me to leave?'

'No, no, this is just a suggestion to save your time,' he replied.

~

We started at 7 a.m. the next morning. At a leisurely pace we moved along the sides of hills. We were likely to bump into people here, Majeed told me. He reminded me to declare my occupation as a teacher were a passer-by to make any inquiries about me. I nodded.

Not ten minutes later, we ran into a distant cousin of Majeed's. Both chatted, embraced each other, and then his cousin looked at me. I panicked and started walking faster. He caught up sooner than I had anticipated.

'So what do you do?'

I said, 'Teacher,' at the same time as Shakil said, '*Akhbaar waala.* [journalist].'

Majeed handled it well. I was a part-timer who dabbled in all sorts of occupations, he said, slowing his pace deliberately to allow Shakil and me to speed past them.

Shakil was quite happy that day. He got to carry the little lamb in his shawl-turned-bag behind his shoulders. I was happy for him. He talked to the lamb at length about this and that. '*Khuch khaaya ki ni khaaya tune . . . Naam kya rakhein tera . . . Koi tang to ni kar raha tereko* [Have you had anything . . . What should we name you . . . Is anyone troubling you]' and so on. I was looking at the nearby hills wondering whether it really was my last day with them. Nazeer couldn't have been more polite, but he couldn't have been clearer in asking me to leave. I was caught up in such thoughts when Shakil shouted at the lamb, '*Arre ye to mutan lag gayo* [The damn thing has started leaking].' I looked up and saw dark threads running down his kurta and shawl. '*Udhar kyun nahi muteya* [Why didn't you pee over there]?' Shakil scolded the lamb. His anger turned the leak into a torrent. Shakil was now boiling with rage. He tried to hit the lamb with his stick. But he couldn't reach the animal who was safely tucked just behind Shakil's neck. '*Le . . . aur le* [Take that . . . take more of it].' He went for the lamb and repeatedly ended up smacking his own ass. I couldn't stop laughing. I had to sit on the floor to catch breath. This was the hardest I had laughed in a long, long time.

On the far, distant right, I saw small clusters of houses on hillsides and a little hairpin bend of a metalled road. The sun had finally come out. After days of feeling damp and cold in sleep and wakefulness, it felt like we were returning from the dark trenches back into civilization. The battered old frame desperately needed some warmth.

Everyone was happy that day. We reached our spot at 9.30 a.m. The horses upturned, the injured white goat was alive and limping. Koka was smiling. Naziya was caressing her dogs. Majeed looked at Saji and Altaf, who were running around with the goats, and, looking at his wife, said, 'Bilkul Ram aur Lacchman ki jodi hai inki [They're together like Lord Ram and Lakshman].' Naseem was cheerful, as was little Haider. He was hiding behind a bush, and as soon as I walked past it, SMACK, he gave me one on the shins with a stick. I stared at him with murderous intent when Riyaz, greatly amused by his boy, picked him up in his arms and took him away.

I pleaded with Majeed and Nazeer to let me walk all the way to their winter stopover. But they didn't think it was a good idea. 'We'll spend, who knows, ten days or twenty days here. What will you do here all this while?' Nazeer said. They were as polite as one could be about showing a guest who has overstayed his welcome the door. That was it then. I thanked everyone. We clicked group photographs. One with all the men and boys, one with all the women and girls, one with the elders and so on. The next morning, I would take the bus out of here, crossing that little hairpin bend.

I went and sat in Nazeer's tent, going through the remaining few pages of Rebecca West's Black Lamb and Grey Falcon. Those were moments of supreme calm. A mild breeze kept nudging the tarpaulin to one side, exposing a beautiful sunlit valley far below. Somewhere in that valley another group of Bakarwals was camping. One could hear faint voices of their children playing cricket. Rashid had gone to them to barter his apples for corn. I knew I would miss him. His 'Aar Ae Ess Etch Eye Dee . . . Rashid'. His playing an adult in front of everyone, and spending a whole day rolling a toy car when he thought no one was watching. I would miss Shaheen and envy her for her confidence and pride. I would miss Mushtaq who dreamed of a better life for his children, Shakil for his playfulness, Koka, Nazeer, Majeed, all of them.

But the person I knew I would spend a lot of time thinking about was Rabeena. She alone, of all the people in that caravan, understood the absurdity of her life. The punishing back-and-forth that would never end. But all this didn't break her. She was like Albert Camus's Sisyphus, who is superior to his fate and stronger than the rock that he keeps pushing up. He 'knows the whole extent of his wretched condition; it is what he thinks of during his descent. The lucidity that was to constitute his torture at the same time crowns his victory'. Sisyphus is like a blind man eager to find out who else knows that the night has no end, Camus said, 'he is still on the go. The rock is still rolling.'

Acknowledgements

This book became possible and gained a lot from the support of many individuals. I owe a lot to Praveen Thampi, whose encouragement came at a crucial time for me.

I am really grateful to my wonderfully talented fellow journalist Aakash Hassan, who repeatedly went out of his way to offer his help. To Safeena Wani and Hakeem Irfan, for those unending discussions and for all their support. They know what they mean to me. I should add here that any mistakes or errors in this book and all the opinions stated in it are solely mine.

It would be impossible to thank Elizabeth Kuruvilla enough for the efforts she put in to turn my first draft into my first book. Her literary judgement often came to my rescue. Equally difficult would be the task of appreciating Shreya Chakravertty for the close attention she paid to the fine print from which the book benefited immensely. And a big thank you to Kanishka. None of this would have been possible had he not believed in me in the first place.

Finally, I would like to express my heartfelt gratitude to all the people of Kashmir who gave me their time, who hosted me and opened up to me in good faith. I'll never be able to repay the debt, especially to my Bakarwal hosts, who accepted me as one of their own and yet extended to me all the privileges of a guest.

Notes

North Kashmir

Chapter 1: Gurez: In the Shadow of the Moon

1. On 5 August 2019, the Indian government scrapped the special status granted to Jammu and Kashmir by amending Article 370 of the Indian Constitution. Subsequently, the state itself was split into two Union Territories: Jammu and Kashmir, and Ladakh—bringing the region directly under the control of New Delhi. Dozens of petitions challenging the Centre's move to abrogate Article 370 are pending in the Supreme Court.
2. Walter R. Lawrence, *The Valley of Kashmir* (Oxford, UK: Oxford University Press, 1895), p. 16.
3. Oscar Eckenstein, *The Karakorams and Kashmir* (Srinagar: Gulshan Books, 1896).
4. Neerja Mattoo, trans., *The Mystic and the Lyric: Four Women Poets from Kashmir* (New Delhi: Zubaan), pp. 92, 94, 129
5. https://www.news18.com/news/india/kashmir-dispatch-6-10-days-10-phone-booths-and-80-lakh-people-waiting-in-queue-2270895.html, News18.com, 15 August 2019.
6. Ibid.
7. https://www.youtube.com/watch?v=7Zw7lelK7Xc&feature=youtu.be, *New Indian Express*, 11 August 2019.

8.   https://www.news18.com/news/india/kashmir-dispatch-4-with-no-means-to-reach-out-to-families-emergency-patients-struggle-alone-in-srinagar-hospital-2265975.html, News18.com, 11 August 2019.

9.   https://www.nytimes.com/2019/10/07/world/asia/kashmir-doctors-phone.html, *New York Times*, 7 October 2019.

Chapter 2: Merry Christmas in Baramulla

1.   *Witness: Kashmir 1986–2016, Nine Photographer*s (New Delhi: Yaarbal, 2017).

2.   George Orwell, *George Orwell: Essays* (London: Penguin, 2000), p. 353.

Chapter 3: The Winds of Sopore

1.   https://www.amnesty.org/download/Documents/188000/asa200171993en.pdf, Amnesty International, April 1993; https://www.greaterkashmir.com/news/kashmir/jan-6-1993-bsf-men-killed-75-civilians-burnt-sopore-market/

Srinagar

Chapter 1: A Walk along the Bund

1.   Rahul Pandita, *Our Moon has Blood Clots: A Memoir of a Lost Home in Kashmir* (Penguin India, 2017, Kindle edition, Loc 2726).

Chapter 2: Sitting by the Jhelum

1.   Aijaz Ahmad Bund, *The Hijras of Kashmir: A Marginalized Form of Personhood* (Srinagar: JayKay Books, 2017).

South Kashmir

Chapter 2: To the Spring of Verinag

1.   Khalid Bashir Ahmad, *Jhelum: The River Through My Backyard* (Srinagar: Gulshan Books, 2012), p. 25.

2. Shonaleeka Kaul, *The Making of Early Kashmir: Landscape and Identity in the Rajatarangini* (OUP India, 2018), p. 72. The author quotes from the Sanskrit epic *Rajatarangini* (River of Kings), on one thousand years of Kashmiri royalty.

Chapter 3: Playing Shakespeare in Mohripora

1. Walter R. Lawrence, *The Valley of Kashmir* (London: H. Frowde, 1895), p. 293.

Chapter 4: The Yeats of Pulwama

1. Kurt Vonnegut, *Letters by Kurt Vonnegut* (Penguin, Kindle edition, 2012).
2. W.H. Auden, 'In Memory of W.B. Yeats', in *Collected Poems: W.H. Auden* (Penguin US, 1990).

Chapter 5: The Old Man of Shopian

1. Ramachandra Guha, 'Gandhi in Kashmir, Gandhians on Kashmir', *Telegraph*, 16 August 2019.
2. Agha Shahid Ali, 'From Amherst to Kashmir', in *The Veiled Suite* (New Delhi: Penguin India, 2009), p. 260.
3. Agha Shahid Ali, 'I See Kashmir from New Delhi at Midnight' in *The Veiled Suite* (New Delhi: Penguin India, 2009), p. 178.
4. Rahul Pandita, *Our Moon Has Blood Clots* (Random House India, 2013), p. 86.
5. Agha Shahid Ali, 'Farewell', in *The Veiled Suite* (New Delhi: Penguin India, 2009), p. 175.
6. V.S. Naipaul, *The Enigma of Arrival* (London: Picador, 1987), p. 93.

A Long Walk with the Bakarwals

1. Rebecca West, *Black Lamb and Grey Falcon* (Penguin Classics US, 1931), p. 2.
2. Walter R. Lawrence, *The Valley of Kashmir* (Srinagar: Gulshan Books, 1895), p. 213.

3. https://www.hindustantimes.com/chandigarh/strained-relations-with-bakarwals-motive-behind-gangrape-and-murder-in-kathua-special-court/story-3KZfkbAtH29PZWlj1KmbZI.html, *Hindustan Times*, 12 June 2019.

4. https://economictimes.indiatimes.com/news/politics-and-nation/hindu-ekta-manch-plan-a-strike-in-hiranagar-of-jammu/articleshow/62983917.cms?from=mdr, *Economic Times*, 19 February 2018.

5. https://www.indiatoday.in/india/story/kathua-rape-case-2-bjp-ministers-attend-rally-in-support-of-accused-1181788-2018-03-04, *India Today*, 4 March 2018.

6. Abul Fazl Allami, *Ain I Akbari* (1873), p. 348.

7. George Orwell, *The Road to Wigan Pier* (Penguin, Kindle edition, Loc 167).

8. V.S. Naipaul, *India: A Wounded Civilisation* (London: Picador, 1976), p. 57.

9. West, *Black Lamb and Grey Falcon*, p. 786.